Ray Bradbury

WHO WROTE THAT?

LOUISA MAY ALCOTT,
   SECOND EDITION
JANE AUSTEN
AVI
L. FRANK BAUM
JUDY BLUME,
   SECOND EDITION
RAY BRADBURY
BETSY BYARS
MEG CABOT
BEVERLY CLEARY
ROBERT CORMIER
BRUCE COVILLE
SHARON CREECH
ROALD DAHL
CHARLES DICKENS
DR. SEUSS,
   SECOND EDITION
ERNEST J. GAINES
S.E. HINTON
WILL HOBBS
ANTHONY HOROWITZ

STEPHEN KING
URSULA K. LE GUIN
MADELEINE L'ENGLE
GAIL CARSON LEVINE
C.S. LEWIS,
   SECOND EDITION
LOIS LOWRY
ANN M. MARTIN
STEPHENIE MEYER
L.M. MONTGOMERY
PAT MORA
WALTER DEAN MYERS
ANDRE NORTON
SCOTT O'DELL
CHRISTOPHER PAOLINI
BARBARA PARK
KATHERINE PATERSON
GARY PAULSEN
RICHARD PECK
TAMORA PIERCE
DAVID "DAV" PILKEY
EDGAR ALLAN POE

BEATRIX POTTER
PHILIP PULLMAN
MYTHMAKER:
   THE STORY OF
   J.K. ROWLING,
   SECOND EDITION
MAURICE SENDAK
SHEL SILVERSTEIN
LEMONY SNICKET
GARY SOTO
JERRY SPINELLI
R.L. STINE
EDWARD L.
   STRATEMEYER
MARK TWAIN
H.G. WELLS
E.B. WHITE
LAURA INGALLS
   WILDER
JACQUELINE WILSON
LAURENCE YEP
JANE YOLEN

Ray Bradbury

John Bankston

Foreword by
Kyle Zimmer

CHELSEA HOUSE
An Infobase Learning Company

Ray Bradbury

Chelsea House
An imprint of Infobase Learning
132 West 31st Street
New York, NY 10001

Library of Congress Cataloging-in-Publication Data
Bankston, John, 1974-
Ray Bradbury / by John Bankston.
p. cm.—(Who wrote that?)
Includes bibliographical references and index.
ISBN 978-1-60413-778-1
1. Bradbury, Ray, 1920—Juvenile literature. 2. Authors, American—20th century—Biography—Juvenile literature. 3. Science fiction—Authorship—Juvenile literature. 4. Fantasy fiction—Authorship—Juvenile literature. I. Title.
PS3503.R167Z57 2011
813'.54—dc22
[B]   2010029477

Chelsea House books are available at special discounts when purchased in bulk quantities for business, associations, institutions, or sales promotions. Please call our Special Sales Department in New York at (212) 967-8800 or (800) 322-8755.

You can find Chelsea House on the World Wide Web at
http://www.infobaselearning.com.

Text design by Keith Trego
Cover design by Alicia Post
Composition by EJB Publishing Services
Cover printed by Yurchak Printing, Landisville, Pa.
Book printed and bound by Yurchak Printing, Landisville, Pa.
Date printed: May 2011
Printed in the United States of America

10 9 8 7 6 5 4 3 2 1

This book is printed on acid-free paper.

All links and Web addresses were checked and verified to be correct at the time of publication. Because of the dynamic nature of the Web, some addresses and links may have changed since publication and may no longer be valid.

Table of Contents

FOREWORD BY
KYLE ZIMMER
PRESIDENT, FIRST BOOK

HUMANITY IS POWERED by stories. From our earliest days as thinking beings, we employed every available tool to tell each other stories. We danced, drew pictures on the walls of our caves, spoke, and sang. All of this extraordinary effort was designed to entertain, recount the news of the day, explain natural occurrences—and then gradually to build religious and cultural traditions and establish the common bonds and continuity that eventually formed civilizations. Stories are the most powerful force in the universe; they are the primary element that has distinguished our evolutionary path.

Our love of the story has not diminished with time. Enormous segments of societies are devoted to the art of storytelling. Book sales in the United States alone topped $24 billion in 2006; movie studios spend fortunes to create and promote stories; and the news industry is more pervasive in its presence than ever before.

There is no mystery to our fascination. Great stories are magic. They can introduce us to new cultures, or remind us of the nobility and failures of our own, inspire us to greatness or scare us to death; but above all, stories provide human insight on a level that is unavailable through any other source. In fact, stories connect each of us to the rest of humanity not just in our own time, but also throughout history.

This special magic of books is the greatest treasure that we can hand down from generation to generation. In fact, that spark in a child that comes from books became the motivation for the creation of my organization, First Book, a national literacy program with a simple mission: to provide new books to the most disadvantaged children. At present, First Book has been at work in hundreds of communities for over a decade. Every year children in need receive millions of books through our organization and millions more are provided through dedicated literacy institutions across the United States and around the world. In addition, groups of people dedicate themselves tirelessly to working with children to share reading and stories in every imaginable setting from schools to the streets. Of course, this Herculean effort serves many important goals. Literacy translates to productivity and employability in life and many other valid and even essential elements. But at the heart of this movement are people who love stories, love to read, and want desperately to ensure that no one misses the wonderful possibilities that reading provides.

When thinking about the importance of books, there is an overwhelming urge to cite the literary devotion of great minds. Some have written of the magnitude of the importance of literature. Amy Lowell, an American poet, captured the concept when she said, "Books are more than books. They are the life, the very heart and core of ages past, the reason why men lived and worked and died, the essence and quintessence of their lives." Others have spoken of their personal obsession with books, as in Thomas Jefferson's simple statement: "I live for books." But more compelling, perhaps, is the almost instinctive excitement in children for books and stories.

Throughout my years at First Book, I have heard truly extraordinary stories about the power of books in the lives of children. In one case, a homeless child, who had been bounced from one location to another, later resurfaced—and the only possession that he had fought to keep was the book he was given as part of a First Book distribution months earlier. More recently, I met a child who, upon receiving the book he wanted, flashed a big smile and said, "This is my big chance!" These snapshots reveal the true power of books and stories to give hope and change lives.

As these children grow up and continue to develop their love of reading, they will owe a profound debt to those volunteers who reached out to them—a debt that they may repay by reaching out to spark the next generation of readers. But there is a greater debt owed by all of us—a debt to the storytellers, the authors, who have bound us together, inspired our leaders, fueled our civilizations, and helped us put our children to sleep with their heads full of images and ideas.

WHO WROTE THAT? is a series of books dedicated to introducing us to a few of these incredible individuals. While we have almost always honored stories, we have not uniformly honored storytellers. In fact, some of the most important authors have toiled in complete obscurity throughout their lives or have been openly persecuted for the uncomfortable truths that they have laid before us. When confronted with the magnitude of their written work or perhaps the daily grind of our own, we can forget that writers are people. They struggle through the same daily indignities and dental appointments, and they experience the intense joy and bottomless despair that many of us do. Yet somehow they rise above it all to deliver a powerful thread that connects us all. It is a rare honor to have the opportunity that these books provide to share the lives of these extraordinary people. Enjoy.

A circa-1950 portrait of Ray Bradbury as a young author. Bradbury first made his reputation with The Martian Chronicles, *a collection of inter-connected stories that relates the experiences of men and women who were among the early arrivals on the red planet.*

A Road Trip

THE TRIP FROM Los Angeles to New York City was nearly 3,000 miles (4,828 kilometers). Ray Bradbury took a bus.

It was 1950. The writer was terrified of planes and automobiles. Besides, air travel was too expensive (and train trips were scarcely better). Although his hometown of Los Angeles had embraced the automobile faster than any other city in the United States, it did not make him more interested in buying one. Even if he decided to make a cross-country road trip, he could not afford a car.

In the mid-twentieth century, cross-country trips were far more arduous than today. U.S. Route 66, now internationally famous, had been constructed in the 1930s. Twenty years later, when Bradbury made his trip, it remained the fastest road from Los Angeles to Chicago; construction on the much swifter Interstate Highway System familiar to modern travelers was still six years away.

When Bradbury boarded a bus in Los Angeles, he had a long trip ahead of him. "So, I got on the Greyhound bus, four days, four nights," he recalled in a speech. "Have you ever done that on the Greyhound bus? Don't. *Don't.* Those were the days before air conditioning and toilets."[1]

Although Bradbury was then becoming known as a science fiction writer, he did not embrace the unquestioning adoration of technological advances often seen in the works of other science fiction writers. Instead, like his contemporaries Robert A. Heinlein, Philip K. Dick, and Andre Norton, Bradbury's stories examined technology's dark side. "To Bradbury, as to most people, radar and rocket ships and atomic power are big, frightening, meaningless names," explained critic Damon Knight. "Bradbury's strength lies in the fact that he writes about the things that are really important to us."[2]

More than 60 years ago, Bradbury was already creating stories concerned about people destroying the environment and decimating native populations. While his writing was not universally anti-tech, he saw the potential for scientific advances to ruin art, damage lives, and even enslave people. In his story "The Earthmen," for example, an early American expedition of Mars ended with the team's murder following internment in an insane asylum. In another Mars-set short story, Bradbury paid homage to his literary hero Edgar Allan Poe. "Usher II" featured a wealthy settler recreating the House of Usher on Mars (from Poe's "The

Fall of the House of Usher"). He then eliminates a censoring Earthling who would have benefited from reading Poe's "The Cask of Amontillado."

SELLING STORIES

Bradbury's writing followed in Poe's tradition of gothic horror. Because his stories were not clearly "sci-fi," many of the magazines he loved as boy rejected stories he submitted to them as an adult. After making a few early sales to *Weird Tales* and *Thrilling Wonder*, he began selling to "the slicks"—popular magazines such as *Mademoiselle*, *Esquire*, the *Saturday Evening Post*, and *American Mercury*.

While the income he made from his short stories was enough to allow him to quit his job as a newspaper deliveryman while in his early twenties, it barely paid the bills. Yet, other than selling newspapers, writing had been his only job. By 1949, he had begun earning awards and an audience, success great enough that his stories were collected in a book titled *Dark Carnival*.

In order to make a decent living, Bradbury knew he needed to sell a novel. In order to do that, he had to go to

Did you know...

Ray Bradbury's first book, *Dark Carnival*, with only 3,000 copies produced, is a sought-after collectible. Depending on the condition, a signed first edition commands between $800 and more than $4,000.

New York, where the major book publishers were located. So without any guarantees, the writer boarded a bus and headed for New York City.

After nearly 100 hours on a bus, Bradbury remembered, "I arrived at the YMCA, the Sloan House, moved in there for $5 a week and proceeded to show my short stories to editors all around New York City, but nobody wanted my short stories. They said, 'Don't you have a novel?' I said, 'No I'm a sprinter.'"[3] They wanted a marathoner— someone who could complete a lengthy novel. For the next week, the young writer kept hearing, "Thanks, but no thanks." Rejection, like paper, is an essential component of most writers' lives, but it cuts more often and more deeply.

On his last night in New York, Bradbury had dinner with an editor who shared his last name. The unrelated Walter Bradbury asked, according to the author, "about all those Martian stories you've been writing in the pulp magazines during the last ten years. Don't you think they would make a novel if you wove them together in some sort of tapestry?"[4]

Ray Bradbury stared at the editor, overwhelmed by the idea's potential. He had read Sherwood Anderson's ground-breaking *Winesburg, Ohio,* half-a-dozen years before. That 1919 novel of interconnected stories led the science fiction writer to think, "Wouldn't it be wonderful if someday I could write a book as good as this but put it on the planet Mars?"[5]

Now he sat across from an editor who stumbled upon the same idea Bradbury had nearly forgotten. Walter Bradbury scheduled a meeting for the next day; if a suitable outline was developed, he would give the writer a contract and money.

Ray Bradbury could not wait to get back to his room. He did not sleep. He wrote, laboring to develop the novel's outline along with short sections to connect the stories.

The next morning, clutching his new material, Bradbury met with Walter Bradbury. In a speech 50 years later, Ray Bradbury remembered the editor's response. "Yes, this is it. Here's $750."[6]

They also agreed to expand one of the writer's short stories about a sea monster into a 50,000-word novel. Editor Bradbury gave writer Bradbury another contract—and another $750. Fifteen hundred dollars was a tremendous amount of money in 1950. "I was rich," he said. "It paid our rent for the next two years. Our rent was only thirty dollars a month. It paid for our baby. Babies were cheap back then. It cost $100 for our baby."[7]

Today, the book he wrote, *The Martian Chronicles*, is considered a milestone in the genre of science fiction. By the time Ray Bradbury had sold this book, he had spent many years developing his talent. He had been preparing for much of his life to be not only a writer but also a successful author. Money from *The Martian Chronicles* altered Ray Bradbury's circumstances. The critical and popular response to it changed his life.

Though originally from Illinois, the Bradbury family twice lived in Tucson, Arizona, during the author's childhood. They eventually settled in Los Angeles, California, when Ray Bradbury was 13 years old. The Arizona deserts likely inspired Bradbury's depiction of Mars in **The Martian Chronicles.**

2

Green Town, Illinois

Waukegan, visited by me often since, is neither homelier nor more beautiful than any other small Midwestern town. Much of it is green. The trees do touch in the middle of streets. The street in front of my old home is still paved with red bricks. In what way then was the town special? Why, I was born there. It was my life. I had to write of it as I saw fit.[1]

—Ray Bradbury

On August 22, 1920, Ray Douglas Bradbury was born to the former Marie Esther Moberg, a native Swede, and her husband, Leonard Spalding Bradbury. The future writer of interstellar journeys got his middle name from earthbound movie star

Douglas Fairbanks. He was delivered a few blocks from the family home at Maternity Hospital in Waukegan, Illinois.

"It all began the day I was born. . . . I remember being born," he claimed in the introduction to his short story collection *The October Country*.

> I found out many, many years later the reason for my remembrance: I was a ten month baby . . . snuggled away for an extra twenty-eight or thirty days I had a serene opportunity to develop my sight, hearing and taste. I came forth wide-eyed, aware of everything I saw and felt. Especially the fearful shock of being propelled out into a cooler environment, leaving my old home forever, to be surrounded by strangers.[2]

Writers with clear memories of early childhood have an advantage over those with more blank spaces than recollections. Childhood stories provide bountiful material. Many authors later describe raw, unhindered emotions, unedited outbursts, and youthful fears of the shape-shifting shadow in a room's corner or the inexplicably ajar closet door spraying light and danger into a child's room. It was no different with young Ray. "I have a feeling my mother infected me," Bradbury later explained. "She was a very fearful woman. I think a lot of her fears were transferred over to me. She was afraid that something might happen to me."[3]

Bradbury's early years were sufficiently unsettled to leave a distinct impression. Stability often creates secure and happy childhoods, but only rarely nurtures successful writers. The best stories require drama. Many of the best writers are forced to disappear into the security of their imaginations as they mature.

In Bradbury's case, tragedy arrived two years before Ray was born. Twins Samuel and Leonard Jr. were born in 1916; but two years later Samuel died, most likely a victim of the Spanish flu pandemic. Ray's sister, Elizabeth, was born in 1926 but succumbed to pneumonia a year later.

SILENT MOVIE INSPIRATIONS

As a toddler, Ray escaped into dark rooms with images projected onto a screen. Three years old and cozy in his mother's lap in a movie theater, he was mesmerized by Lon Chaney's portrayal of the title role in *The Hunchback of Notre Dame*, "riding the bells and raining hot liquid lead on the villains below the church."[4]

He did not see the movie again until he was 17. "I told my friends I remembered the entire film, last seen when I was three. They snorted and laughed. I described the most important scenes. We then went in and there were all the scenes I had described."[5]

Bradbury also claims to have early memories of such early film classics as *The Phantom of the Opera* and *The Lost World*. *The Lost World*'s dinosaurs inspired his short story about a solitary dinosaur that was later adapted into the movie *The Beast from 20,000 Fathoms*. "You pose the question, What if I had given up on dinosaurs?" he later asked. "I wouldn't have had my career."[6]

The movies he saw represented film studios' early efforts to employ special effects and make-up to enthrall and terrify the audience. Although often called "silent movies," live piano music or even orchestras usually accompanied these films when they were shown in theaters. The age of "talkies"—movies that offered synchronous dialogue where characters can be both seen and heard speaking—was ushered in by *The Jazz Singer* in 1927. Before that, title cards, projected on the screen, provided limited dialogue. Everything else had to be expressed by images and the actor's faces.

Ray did not need words to be transported. When the lights dimmed, his imagination was unfettered. Years later, writing to author Stephen King, Bradbury confessed, "I was a raving film maniac long before I hit my eighth year."[7]

In 1926, the family moved to Tucson, Arizona, because Leonard Bradbury believed his family could make a better life for themselves out west. The western edges of the United States have long been associated with reinvention and new opportunities. Some built fortunes after westward moves, but troubles followed many others.

Why did the family move to Tucson? "Beginning in the 1920s, Tucson was promoted in national publications as a tourist destination," notes one study. "The marketing efforts emphasized the city's charm and quaintness and easy access to nearby dude ranches, western ghost towns and Indian Villages. The Hispanic cultural traditions of the barrios and the Old Pueblo image were also included as part of the advertising campaigns."[8]

Lacking the abusive winters and the settled roots of the Middle West, Arizona seemed ideal to Leonard Bradbury. Its bleak landscape, barren of all but the heartiest plants, made a strong impression on his youngest son's developing imagination. During the day, the sun-bleached terrain stretched 100 miles (160.9 kilometers) to the horizon. At dusk, the sand glowed from the setting sun's ruby tinge. After nightfall, stars did not compete with urban lights; the sky's black bowl seemed to reveal the entire universe.

Living in Arizona clearly influenced Bradbury's descriptions of Mars. "Outside, the immense blue Martian sky was hot and still as a warm deep sea water," he wrote in *The Martian Chronicles*. "The Martian desert lay broiling

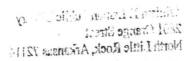

like a prehistoric mud pot, waves of heat rising and shimmering."[9]

Unfortunately, the Bradbury family's first excursion to Arizona ended after only a year. Leonard Bradbury could not find work.

A LOVE OF READING

Although movies were Ray's first love as a boy, he began reading comics in the newspaper when he was six. The Bradbury family did not have money for luxuries, and books were considered luxuries. Accompanied by his older brother, Ray ran to the library at least once a week. Just half a mile (804 meters) from his house, in downtown Waukegan, the stone-and-granite building initiated a lifelong love of libraries in him. "I inundated myself at the library," he remembered. "I plunged in and I drowned. When I visited the library, suddenly the outside world didn't exist. I found a lot of books and I would sit down at the table and drown in them."[10]

He found books on dinosaurs and magic. He secretly read books from the Nancy Drew series—embarrassed to be reading "girl" books but not so embarrassed that he did not read them. On the shelves of his grandparents' library, he discovered L. Frank Baum's Oz series, Lewis Carroll's *Alice's Adventures in Wonderland*, and Edgar Allan Poe's *Tales of Mystery and Imagination*.

He also became a huge fan of science fiction and fantasy magazines. One such magazine, *Amazing Stories*, featured covers depicting enormous ants or stories on rockets and life on other worlds. It was the first of many pulp magazines—so-called because of the cheap paper upon which they were printed—to become a regular part

As a boy, Ray Bradbury devoured science fiction pulp magazines. Here, the cover of the August 1927 issue of Amazing Stories *illustrates a war between humans and giant robots with tentacle-like arms and features stories by H.G. Wells, A. Hyatt Verrill, and Julian Huxley.*

of Ray's reading. Author Robert Heinlein described the unique love readers of such magazines have for the genre: "You leave one around loose in your home and a friend will pick it up. Those who are not fans ask if you really read that stuff, and from then on they look at you with suspicion."[11]

Such magazines were not read by "respectable" people. Ray soon decided other people's opinions mattered far less than what he enjoyed, so he read widely of whatever stories he enjoyed the most. Yet one of his greatest influences was neither a movie nor a book. It was a comic strip: *Buck Rogers in the 25th Century*, which imagined a world of jet packs and rocket trips to Mars and Jupiter. Such a future was an ideal escape when the present was proving to be unrelentingly harsh.

The first decade of Bradbury's life was known as "The Roaring Twenties," a booming time of easy money. It all came to a sudden halt in October 1929. As Matthew J. Bruccoli noted in his introduction to *The Great Gatsby*, F. Scott Fitzgerald's classic novel of the era, "The Twenties was a time of stock market speculation. . . . On 3 September 1929 the Dow Jones Industrial Average [a stock index of major corporations] reached a high of 381; it fell to 261 on 28 October. (It reached a low of 41 in 1932.)"[12]

Over the next 10 years, in a period now known as the Great Depression, unemployment soared past 25 percent, banks and businesses failed, and stocks continued to decline. The stock market did not reach its pre-crash level again until the 1950s. In the Bradbury household, money was always tight, but the Depression only made it worse. As a result of the tough times, escapist fantasies—whether musicals or screwball comedies or fantasy comic strips

Did you know...

Pulp magazines such as *Amazing Stories* and *Wonder Stories* became popular in the late-nineteenth century. Reading was then becoming a popular pastime. The Industrial Revolution's need for educated workers and the spread of compulsory primary education (and increasing numbers of students in optional secondary schools) meant that more people knew how to read. Magazines and cheaply printed novels appeared to meet a growing demand. In 1896, the first pulp, *Argosy*, promised 192 pages of fiction for 10 cents. As readers sought category, or genre, fiction, 1915's *Detective Story Monthly*, 1919's *Western Story Magazine*, and 1926's *Amazing Stories* then appeared.*

While most pulp-genre magazines stopped publishing decades ago, several science fiction pulps have survived. *Analog Science Fiction and Fact*, which began as *Astounding Stories of Super Science* in 1938 under the editorship of John Campbell, continues to be published. *The Magazine of Fantasy and Science Fiction* has been produced since 1949. *Amazing Stories* endured until the 1990s and inspired a television series produced by Steven Spielberg. Efforts to revive the title in 2003 failed after a year.

*James Gunn, "The Origins of Science Fiction," *The Science of Science Fiction Writing* (Lanham, Md.: The Scarecrow Press, 2000), p. 68.

such as *Buck Rogers in the 25th Century*—were commonly enjoyed.

Bradbury clipped every *Buck Rogers* he read, treasuring them. It was the first collection for a lifelong collector. Then one day, some children his own age teased him for liking "baby stuff," depicting a future they did not believe would ever happen. At home, he furiously tore the strips into shreds.

He soon regretted his actions. The race to grow up was not a competition he wanted to join. "How is it that the boy I was in October of 1929 could . . . tear up his Buck Rogers comic strips and a month later judge all of his friends idiots and rush back to collecting?" he asked in *Zen in the Art of Writing*. "Where did I find the courage to rebel, change my life, live alone? I don't want to over-estimate all this, but . . . I love that nine year old. Without him, I could not have survived."[13]

DISCOVERING MARS

One family bookshelf yielded its own treasure. Uncle Bion Bradbury was a fan of writer Edgar Rice Burroughs, who is today known for two notable series: the adventure tales depicting Tarzan, a man raised by apes, and a series of books set on Mars featuring a Civil War veteran named John Carter.

Ray spent the summer of 1930 running between his house and his uncle's. Then, one sad day, he realized he had read every one of Burroughs's Mars novels. "I couldn't wait the year until the next book came out. . . . I sat down with my friend Bill Arno, and we got out a roll of butcher paper and wrote and illustrated a sequel to *The Gods of Mars*. . . . I launched right into the novel writing business at the start of my career."[14]

RETURN TO TUCSON

In 1932, after several years living back in Illinois, the Bradbury family returned to Tucson. On the way the family stopped at motels. After one stop, Ray ran to the nearest library. He recalled that "the first thing I looked for were the *Oz* books. They weren't there. The second thing I looked for were the Edgar Rice Burroughs *Tarzan* books or his Martian books. They weren't there. . . . It wasn't censorship. It was taste. The librarians looked down their noses at these books—which were not 'literature.' "[15]

In Tucson, Ray cultivated his developing loves: writing and performing. At home, he began working on short stories. At school, he landed a leading role in *A Wooden Shoe Christmas*. He then boldly told friends he was going to work at KGR, a radio station a few blocks from his house—despite not having a job there at the time. This would become a regular habit for Ray Bradbury, predicting events before they took place and then making them happen.

After a few weeks of doing odd jobs at the station, Ray was asked if he wanted to be on the air. (In these pre-television years, comedies and dramas were heard on radio. Regular viewers tuned in to their favorite stories just as television audiences do today.) He began by reading Sunday comics on air and adding sound effects for live broadcasts.

He loved the job and imagined a career for himself in radio. When his father announced the family's return to Illinois, Ray was heartbroken. On his last day, the radio announcer said goodbye to him over the air. This time, however, the Bradbury family's time in Waukegan was brief. In 1934, the family moved once more and for the last time. Their new home would be Ray Bradbury's home for the next 70 years. Sometimes called "the dream factory," it remains a destination for thousands of star-struck hopefuls: Los Angeles.

A circa-1930s photo of Paramount Studios in Hollywood, California. As a boy, Ray Bradbury used to roller skate down to the studio to see famous radio and film stars, including George Burns and Gracie Allen.

3

L.A. Dreaming

DURING THE BOOM YEARS of the 1920s, Los Angeles County's population nearly doubled, reaching more than 2 million. The Great Depression scarcely slowed the influx. In 1936, in fact, 130 L.A. police officers were dispatched to the Nevada-California border in an effort to prevent unemployed hitchhikers from seeking transit and work. It did little to stem the tide.

Ray Bradbury's family was similar to many others who arrived in Los Angeles during the 1930s. After moving his family into a cramped apartment at 1318 Hobart Avenue, Leonard Bradbury spent weeks struggling to find work. The first time

Ray saw his father cry was after his sister's death. The second was when his father thought the family would have to return to Illinois. Shortly afterward, the General Cable Company hired the elder Bradbury as a lineman. It was a blessing for both father and son, as Ray had already fallen in love with the city.

Arriving in April, the Bradbury brothers convinced their parents that the school year ended in a few weeks (it actually ended in mid-June). Since such an abbreviated semester seemed pointless, they enjoyed an extended summer. Ray began roller-skating the short distance from his apartment to Paramount Studios. There he earned an autograph from the comedic actor W.C. Fields. He even persuaded movie star Marlene Dietrich to cross a street where the lighting was better for a picture!

When he began ninth grade at Berendo Junior High School, Ray was already a familiar sight outside the Figueroa Playhouse, where many film stars could be found. There, Ray met comedian George Burns. Born in 1896, Burns was

Did you know...

A great movie fan, Ray Bradbury lists a number of films that inspired him growing up. They include *Robin Hood* (1922), *The Phantom of the Opera* (1925), *The Skeleton Dance* (1929), *King Kong* (1933), *Things to Come* (1936), and *Fantasia* (1940).*

*Sam Weller, *The Bradbury Chronicles: The Life of Ray Bradbury* (New York: Harper Perennial, 2005), pp. 10–11.

performing professionally by the time he was seven. Stardom arrived when he was in his twenties and dating an unemployed, 17-year-old actress named Gracie Allen. Married in 1926, they began as a comedy duo with Burns telling the jokes and Allen playing the "straight man." After realizing the act was funnier when he was the one playing straight to Allen's unusual remarks, the couple switched roles. They also transitioned seamlessly between mediums. Burns and Allen acted in movies for Paramount, then spent 21 years on radio and another eight on television. Following Allen's death in 1964, Burns's star faded. He then enjoyed a career resurgence in the 1970s, beginning with *The Sunshine Boys* in 1975 and by playing the title role in 1977's *Oh, God!* He died in 1996, a few months after turning 100 years old.

In 1934, Burns and Allen's radio show was broadcast at the Playhouse. One day, as Bradbury told biographer Sam Weller, he "skated up to convince [Burns] that he should take me and my friend Donald Harkins in to watch their rehearsals." He continued, "Why George agreed, I'll never know. Perhaps we looked as poor and pitiful as we truly were."[1]

Although rehearsals for radio shows did not usually have an audience, Ray and his friend sat in the front row while the comedy duo performed. Ray had volunteered for "audience work," a job that struggling actors are now paid for, usually minimum wage. Today, they populate the best-dressed first two rows of struggling talk shows and laugh the loudest during the least popular sitcoms. Though unpaid, Ray's participation offered something more important: access.

A year later, while attending Los Angeles High School, Ray spent his time in typing class writing comedy routines.

He recalled that Burns "told me I was a genius and the scripts were brilliant. Of course they were lousy and he knew that but he was polite." Burns eventually used a short bit to close one show.[2]

ERRORS AND TRIALS

At 16, Ray's writing career was beginning to blossom. He had a poem published in the *Waukegan News-Sun*. Observing the one-year anniversary of humorist Will Rogers' death in a plane crash, it began "The man who jested all his life, and chased away all care and strife."[3] He also discovered another profound influence through his reading. Although Jules Verne, Edgar Rice Burroughs, and Edgar Allan Poe had appeared on Ray's reading list for years, he did not begin reading nineteenth-century British author H.G. Wells until high school. "[Wells] was very negative but very exciting because when you're sixteen, you're paranoid, and H.G. Wells is a very paranoid writer," he said. "And a very necessary one."[4]

A college dropout, Wells was a moderately successful journalist when he penned the novels that have endured more than a century after their initial publication. He dubbed his novels *The Time Machine*, *The Invisible Man*, and *The War of the Worlds* "scientific romances." As *Contemporary Authors Online* notes, "He produced an average of nearly three books a year for more than fifty years . . . from fiction to history to science, social activism, literary criticism, biography and film. Altogether, Wells penned more words than William Shakespeare and Charles Dickens combined."[5]

While Wells felt his later nonfiction works championing socialism were his greatest contributions to literature, it was

The British author H.G. Wells, considered one of the fathers of science fiction, was one of Ray Bradbury's early inspirations. His most famous works include The Time Machine *(1895),* The Invisible Man *(1897), and* The War of the Worlds *(1898).*

instead the novels that he considered lightweight which are still read and in print. When his "scientific romances" were reprinted in the first issues of *Amazing Stories* in 1926, Wells was called "the father of modern science fiction."[6]

The range of Wells' work appealed to young Ray, who came to believe that a writer's reach should exceed his grasp. "Go to the edge of a cliff and jump off," he later advised. "Build your wings on the way down."[7] As a teen, Ray embraced this philosophy by submitting his first short stories to major national magazines. His writing was raw, purple, and clearly imitated his literary heroes. "While it's a fair job," an *Esquire* editor wrote rejecting Ray's submission, "the idea is one of those that is constantly occurring."[8]

Ray also submitted to a magazine his father read and admired, the *Saturday Evening Post*. Begun as Benjamin Franklin's *Pennsylvania Gazette* in 1728, it was renamed the *Saturday Evening Post* in 1821. At the time Ray submitted one of his stories, it had become the first magazine to have a monthly circulation exceeding one million. His was one of thousands of unsolicited manuscripts the magazine received. The odds were slim that it would publish him, since even well-known authors were often rejected.

Yet the aspiring writer refused to allow rejection letters to slow him down, maintaining a schedule of writing and submitting one story a week. "I just figured the editors didn't know what they were doing," he remembered later.[9]

CHURCH OF BRADBURY

Because writing is such a solitary endeavor, successful authors usually recommend having support systems. "An occupational hazard of writing is that you'll have bad days," explains Anne Lamott in her book on writing, *Bird by Bird.* "But if you talk to other people who write, you remember that this feeling is part of the process, that it's inevitable."[10] Although *Bird by Bird* was written years later, Bradbury seemingly agrees with this thinking. "If I were to give advice to young writers," Ray Bradbury offered in a 1961 lecture at UCLA, "I would say, 'Number one, they should start writing every day of their lives. Number two, they should go out and seek other people in a similar situation—find an ad hoc church, you might say.'"[11]

In 1937, Ray responded to a handbill for the Science Fiction Society. Founded the year before by 20-year-old Forrest J. Ackerman, the group met regularly on the third floor of Clifton's Cafeteria in downtown Los Angeles. "I bought myself a ten-cent malt," Ray remembered of the first meeting he attended, "and went upstairs and I looked in the room at all these weird people."[12]

He became a regular at the one-hour lectures, interacting with gifted amateurs and working professionals. Sometimes loud, usually precocious, Ray was very opinionated. Adults who sold their writing were generally disinterested in the advice of someone both unpublished and in high school. "Ray was a rather boisterous boy," Ackerman remembered. "He liked to imitate Hitler and W.C. Fields. It's a wonder we didn't strangle him." He also recalled that Ray also had "an overwhelming enthusiasm about his work."[13]

"The group changed my life," Bradbury later noted. "They took me in. I was nowhere, I had nowhere to go. They gave me focus."[14] The group even prompted his first major professional expense. Although his father bought him a toy typewriter while in grade school, it was not suitable for submissions. A member of the society sold him a typewriter on a payment plan of a dollar a week. Without an income or an allowance, Ray was forced to skip the lunch he paid a quarter for every day.

Having the proper equipment (and eventually learning to type more than 100 words per minute) did not provide immediate success. It was not just an inability to sell a story; he was challenged to even get a fiction piece accepted by his high school literary magazine, *Los Angeles High School Fiction*. Despite multiple submissions, Ray's stories never appeared in the publication.

He was mainly writing science fiction stories, a genre many looked down upon and few understood. Others, however, encouraged him. His short story teacher, Jennet Johnson, noted, "I don't know what it is you're doing, but don't stop."[15] Another teacher who encouraged him was poetry teacher Snow Longley Housh, who admired Ray's early poetry. (Bradbury later dedicated a novel to his high school teachers Housh and Johnson.) Besides appearing in the school's poetry magazine, Ray wrote nonfiction pieces for his school paper, *The Blue and White Daily*.

His talents also found an outlet on the stage. He joined his school theater group, the L.A. Players, as a junior, writing and producing his school's annual talent show *The Roman Revue*. It earned a repeat performance, a first for the school.

In 1938, Ray Bradbury graduated from high school with straight A's. He also placed his short story "Hollerbochen's Dilemma" in *Imagination!*, the Science Fiction Society's fanzine. He was not paid, but it was still a milestone.

"Ray was a suffering soul in high school," remembered a fellow writing student at L.A. High, Bonnie Wolf. "He had this burning ambition and at that time it really wasn't based on anything. That was a source for a great deal of despair on his part. At that age, you don't really have any material."[16]

Before Ray Bradbury found success as an author of science fiction and fantasy stories, he made his living selling newspapers. He first sold short stories to pulp magazines and later to larger magazines with a wider readership.

4

Apprenticeship

RAY BRADBURY PAID $80 dollars to secure his first job. It was a tremendous amount of money in 1938; it took loans from his brother and his father to scrape the money together. Still, for an aspiring writer the job was perfect. He would be a newspaper salesman for the *Los Angeles Herald Examiner*'s afternoon edition, the *Herald Express*.

No longer forced to rise at seven in the morning for school, Bradbury gratefully slept past nine. Once awake, he wrote until the early afternoon. Then he made his way to Olympic and Norton avenues, where the bundles of newspapers were dropped off at 4 P.M. As a newspaper salesman, Bradbury quickly abandoned the clichéd call of "Extra! Extra! Read all about it!" "I experimented to see if I shut up, I would sell just as many papers and I did," he told biographer Sam Weller. "People either want a newspaper or they don't."[1]

With his papers usually sold in two hours, Bradbury had sufficient time to devote to his developing craft—one of the most important things a writer can have. As Natalie Goldberg notes in her book *Writing Down the Bones*, "I feel very rich when I have time to write and very poor when I get a regular paycheck and no time to work at my real work."[2]

Bradbury enjoyed his job, not only for its freedom but the chance to interact with people. Bob Gorman, who sold the *L.A. Daily News*, recalled that Bradbury "talked a lot about when he would go into Hollywood and the [movie stars] he would meet." Gorman, however, also felt sorry for the 18-year-old who traveled by roller skates, "While a lot of other young kids were driving automobiles, he never learned how to drive."[3]

Bradbury did not want to learn. At 15, he witnessed the aftermath of a terrible collision. A car had hit a telephone pole, its occupants thrown onto the street. Three people were already dead when he arrived. The fourth, a woman, her face destroyed, died as he watched. "About once a month," the author confessed in the early 2000s, "I still have nightmares about that poor woman who looked at me."[4]

Like many writers, Bradbury dealt with his fears by writing. In "The Crowd," the story's narrator, Spallner, observes groups quickly gathering around auto accidents, no matter the time of day or night. He recognizes the same faces in "the crowd," and a victim similar to the one Bradbury saw as a teen: "She's dying," the narrator hears, "She'll be dead before the ambulance arrives. They shouldn't have moved her. . . ." Spallner relates this to his friend, "They moved her, Morgan, someone moved her. You should never move a traffic victim. It kills them." Spallner realizes "the crowd" is not just witnessing death, but hastening it.[5]

Despite his fears, Bradbury had an advantage over most 18-year-olds: He knew what he wanted to do and what he did not. In early 1939, he was accepted into Los Angeles City College. Though prepared to attend classes, he changed his mind at the last moment. He realized there was nothing he wanted there, except an easier way to meet girls. That was not enough.

Bradbury then decided to embark on the nontraditional journey of an autodidact, or self-taught person. He made extensive use of Los Angeles' public libraries and attended Science Fiction Society lectures led by authors such as Robert Heinlein and scientists such as Jack Parsons, who discussed the science of space travel.

SELF-PUBLISHING

Bradbury also guaranteed his short stories publication by starting a magazine. Begun with a loan from Science Fiction Society founder, Forrest Ackerman, *Futuria Fantasia* survived just four issues but proved an enormous educational experience for the young writer. As publisher, editor, and primary contributor, Bradbury used pseudonyms along with his own name to create the illusion of multiple contributors. He was also responsible for selling-out each 100-issue run.

Representing *Futuria Fantasia*, Bradbury attended the inaugural World Science Fiction Convention in New York City, thanks to another loan from Ackerman. Traveling alone on a cross-country bus trip, he studied his *Hartraampf's Vocabulary* book. The work was a negative influence, as it encouraged him to use unfamiliar words. As a young writer, he admits, he fell into the trap that ensnares many novice authors, utilizing unusual, complex words hoping to sound "literary." Most professional editors and authors tend to avoid such a style. In the famous writing style guide *The Elements of Style*, authors William Strunk Jr. and E.B. White advise:

> Rich ornate prose is hard to digest, generally unwholesome and sometimes nauseating. . . . Do not overwrite. . . . Avoid fancy words. . . . If you admire fancy words, if every sky is beauteous, every blonde curvaceous, every intelligent child prodigious, if you are tickled by discombobulate, you will have a bad time.[6]

When Bradbury attended the 1939 debut of the World Science Fiction Convention, it was unlike any event that

Did you know...

Ray Bradbury lists a number of books that inspired him in childhood, including H.G. Wells' *The Invisible Man*, Thomas Wolfe's *Of Time and the River*, and Sherwood Anderson's *Winesburg, Ohio.**

*Sam Weller, *The Bradbury Chronicles: The Life of Ray Bradbury* (New York: Harper Perennial, 2005), pp. 9–10.

had preceded it. It inspired numerous other conventions, including the famous San Diego Comic-Con International. Prior to the WorldCon, science fiction fans felt isolated and rarely gathered in numbers beyond a few dozen; yet in its inaugural year, more than 2,000 people attended WorldCon. There, Ackerman started a trend when he and his girlfriend appeared in costumes inspired by the H.G. Wells novel *The Shape of Things to Come*. Soon myriad conventions hosted fans attired as aliens, space travelers, and the like.

Along with seeking writing jobs and *Future Fantasia* material, Bradbury attended the conference as his friend Hans Bok's agent, selling his drawings to *Weird Tales* magazine. Unfortunately, no one at the convention was interested in Bradbury's own work.

On the return trek, Bradbury stayed in Waukegan for a few days. Spotting John Steinbeck's *The Grapes of Wrath* in a United Cigar store window, he purchased the novel about a poor family from Oklahoma going to California in an attempt to survive the Great Depression. "I got on the Greyhound bus and I went west on the same Route 66 that the Okies took going to California," Bradbury recalled. "Can you imagine a better circumstance to read that book? I was out of my mind!"[7]

DEFINING SCI-FI

Back in Los Angeles, Bradbury continued reading a variety of books, including works by Henry James and Thomas Wolfe. He also read science texts. His lack of classroom time beyond high school, however, contributed to the difficulty he had selling his stories to science fiction magazines. Editors of sci-fi magazines expected submissions to be somewhat grounded in scientific fact. Scientific knowledge helped to distinguish these stories from other genres of fiction. In the *Science of Science Fiction Writing*, James Gunn notes:

> Humanity has tried many strategies for knowing. . . . Science is the strategy invented by Western Civilization beginning about the time of the Renaissance and accelerated by the Industrial Revolution and the Age of Enlightenment. The science strategy involves rational investigation and the development of theories supported by reproducible results. This is the strategy incorporated in SF [science fiction].[8]

Traditional fiction concerns the rules of life and how characters struggle to learn what those rules are and how to live with them—or outside them. In science fiction, Gunn explains, the "rules may not make sense, are incomplete or are inappropriate for this new situation. SF is about new situations, which is why I call it 'the literature of discontinuity.'"[9]

While the fantasy genre also explores discontinuity, Gunn distinguishes fantasy from science fiction, noting that in fantasy a rule of life is altered without reason. For example, the reader completely suspends disbelief in order to enjoy a vampire or dragon story since such creatures do not exist. In science fiction, however, the reader accepts, according to Gunn, "only that the world has been changed by an unusual but natural event." Therefore, fantasy is the "literature of difference" and science fiction is the "literature of change."[10] Bradbury's early work inhabited a thin border between the fantasy and science fiction genres. His stories incorporated details familiar to science fiction fans but rarely applied understood scientific principles.

Hugo Gernsbeck founded several popular science magazines, including *Science and Invention*, before publishing the first pulp Bradbury ever read, *Amazing Stories*.

Designed to be "a charming romance of science intermingled with scientific fact and prophetic vision," it reflected Gernsbeck's belief that "scientifiction" needed to increase the reader's knowledge of science and technology.[11]

Gernsbeck's competitor John W. Campbell shared this belief. After taking over editorship of *Astounding Stories of Super Science*, Campbell shifted its focus from adventure stories in exotic locals to stories set in important scientific places because he believed "good science fiction is based on knowledgeable scientific extrapolation and cannot be inconsistent with known science."[12]

Most science fiction editors and readers shared Campbell's requirements. "There is only one type of story in the world. Your story," Bradbury argued in *Zen in the Art of Writing*. ". . . I have always tried to write my own story. Give it a label if you wish, call it science fiction or fantasy or the mystery or the western. But, at heart, all good stories are the one kind of story, the story written by an individual man from his individual truth."[13]

ACTING UP

Bradbury loved writing but he remained curious about acting. Reading a piece in the newspaper about actress Laraine Day's new theater group, he announced to fellow society members his intention to join the Wilshire Players. Bradbury arrived with notes, manuscripts, and stories in hopes of offering his playwriting services, but Day initially rebuffed him. "Please, you've got to let me in your group because I've told all my friends that you did," he begged.[14]

Touched by his honesty, Day, the future star of Alfred Hitchcock's *Foreign Correspondent*, allowed Bradbury to join. He added jokes to scripts, painted sets, and eventually landed a small part in a play written by Day, *Lame Brains and Daffodils*. Unfortunately the Wilshire Players and the Science Fiction Society both met on Thursday evenings. For a while, Bradbury only attended society meetings whenever Day's group did not meet.

A regular speaker at society meetings was Robert Heinlein who seemed vastly older and worldly wise to most other members. A naval officer discharged for medical reasons, he was 32 when his first story was published in a 1939 issue of *Astounding!* With editor Campbell's guidance, he published four novels in three years along with so many short stories that he found it necessary to use pseudonyms, or pen names.

Bradbury was overwhelmed when the older man befriended him. Heinlein even allowed the younger writer to watch him write. In 1940, Heinlein felt he could find a home for Bradbury's short story, "It's Not the Heat, It's the Hu . . ." about a man who hates clichés. He submitted it to his friend Rob Wagner who edited *Script*, an L.A. literary magazine.

It was not a fanzine like *Imagination*, but it paid the same: *nothing*. Still, it was a professional publication. While Bradbury could have felt more like a hobbyist than a pro, he saw the acceptance as a sign. He stopped publishing *Future Fantasia*. He renewed his focus on writing short stories. Surely he would be paid for something he wrote, sooner rather than later.

In September 1939, German forces invaded Poland, sparking the outbreak of World War II in Europe. Here, a German heavy gun is in position on the outskirts of Warsaw, Poland. The war would change many things, including the trajectory of science fiction and fantasy literature in the postwar years.

5

War!

RAY BRADBURY COULD not escape the bulldog. Dark and vicious, it chased the hapless writer relentlessly. With one swift movement it opened its enormous jaws and swallowed the writer whole.

Awakening, Bradbury realized he had died in his dream. It was 1936; he was certain the dream was a vision of war.

Across the Atlantic Ocean, another world war was about to begin. Having living through the First World War and now enduring the Great Depression, few in the United States were interested in again becoming involved with a European war. While the Depression was difficult in many countries, following World War I, Germany had lost enormous amounts of territory while being required to compensate countries it had attacked. Paying this expense, along with poor economic policy, helped to produce extremely high inflation throughout Germany.

In 1923, Adolf Hitler tried and failed to overthrow the German government in the so-called Munich Beer Hall Putsch. Imprisoned for nine months for his participation, Hitler spent the time writing *Mein Kampf* (German for "My Struggle"). The book described a unified Germany and Austria led by Aryans—a super race of blue-eyed blondes envisioned by the dark-haired, dark-eyed Hitler.

Following his release, Hitler campaigned for the National Socialist German Worker's Party, also known as the Nazi Party. If they gained power, the Nazis promised to curb inflation and increase employment. They also blamed Jews for Germany's problems. Their message found an audience. In 1933, the Nazis won the majority of seats in the German parliament, the Reichstag; their leader, Hitler, was appointed chancellor of Germany. Then, after a suspicious fire leveled the Reichstag, the Nazi-led government granted Hitler emergency powers. He restricted freedom of speech, freedom of the press, and the right of assembly. The opposition was imprisoned. The free movement of German Jews was curtailed, their businesses and homes taken from them.

All of these policies were intended to "purify" Germany of non-Aryans—not only Jews but also Catholics, Romani (also known as Gypsies), Soviet prisoners of war, Polish and Soviet civilians, homosexuals, the disabled, Jehovah's Witnesses, and other political and religious opponents. These people were executed as part of Hitler's "Final Solution." The Nazis systematically killed an estimated

11 million to 17 million people, including more than 6 million European Jews.

Germany's return as a world power required renewed military might. The Treaty of Versailles, signed after World War I, had limited the German army to 100,000 soldiers while outlawing military aircraft, submarines, and tanks. Upon coming to power, Hitler quickly violated these terms as his army trained in Blitzkrieg, or "lightning war." Utilizing fast-moving infantry troops, armored tanks, and air support to crush opposition, Hitler's reconstituted army invaded nations he believed were rightfully Germany territories, such as Czechoslovakia and Poland. In 1938, the Nazi government again violated the treaty by annexing Austria under the German flag. Hitler's invasion of Poland in September 1939 would be the last straw for European powers such as Great Britain and France, which declared war on the Nazi regime with the intent of stopping Hitler from conquering all of Europe.

Not all powers were opposed to Hitler. Like Germany, Italy was controlled by a charismatic fascist leader who restricted freedoms, Benito Mussolini. Emperor Hirohito called for a similar return to national pride for Japan. All three countries—known as the Axis powers—achieved their objectives by military might and invasion. In a single day, May 10, 1940, Hitler's lightning war crushed the combined opposing armies of Belgium, France, and Holland.

For Ray Bradbury, barely in his twenties, the stories in the papers he sold and the movie newsreels he saw were not distant conflicts. If the United States joined the war, he could be drafted. He was convinced if that happened he would be killed—and that the hundreds of stories he had yet to tell would die with him. "I was scared that I would never get a chance to live for my country," Bradbury later told a biographer. "People don't ever talk about that. I wanted to live so I could contribute."[1]

THE ART AND THE CRAFT

His concern at the time might have seemed misplaced. At 21, Bradbury had yet to earn one dollar for his writing. Yet he still approached his craft with a seasoned professional's dedication. In 1941, he rented an office in a rundown building close to where he sold newspapers. After his papers were sold, he went every afternoon to the office, aspiring to complete a story a week.

Bradbury usually finished his rough draft on a Monday; each successive day he would retype it, polishing the story with every draft. After writing every day, he mailed the sixth and final draft every Saturday to publishers. This soon established a pattern. He submitted. Publishers rejected. In 1941, he wrote 52 stories. Only three were eventually published. Biographer David Mogen asserts, Bradbury "feels he could not have written the publishable stories without the experience and self-knowledge gained writing the others."[2]

"I grew up reading and loving the traditional ghost stories of Dickens, Lovecraft, Poe, and later, Kuttner, Bloch and Clark Ashton Smith," Bradbury wrote in *Zen in the Art of Writing*. "I tried to write stories heavily influenced by various of these writers, and succeeded in making quadruple-layered mud pies, all language and style, that would not float and sank without a trace."[3]

The stories he wrote were not hard science fiction, unlike the tales written by his associates. "Ray Bradbury has always considered himself a fantasy writer rather than a science fiction author," biographer Sam Weller notes in *The Bradbury Chronicles.* "'Science fiction,' Ray stated, 'is the art of the possible. Fantasy is the art of the impossible.'"[4] Bradbury would *not* be pigeonholed. He wrote stories that moved him emotionally, stories he enjoyed. "If you are writing without zest, without gusto, without love, without fun, you are only half a writer," Bradbury wrote in *Zen.*[5]

This advice to write what one loves, not what one feels will sell or please the critics, is echoed by another highly successful author, Stephen King, a longtime Bradbury fan. In his book *On Writing*, King noted, "What would be very wrong, I think, is to turn away from what you know and like . . . in favor of things you believe will impress your friends, relatives and writing circle colleagues. What's equally wrong is the deliberate turning toward some genre or type of fiction in order to make money."[6]

Henry Hasse was in his late twenties and the author of a novelette titled "He Who Shrank" when he began collaborating with Ray Bradbury. In 1941, they improved the short story "Pendulum," which first appeared in *Futuria Fantasia*. That story convinced Julius Schwartz (whom Bradbury had met at the first WorldCon) to represent him. On July 18, Schwartz sold the story to *Super Science Stories*. The magazine paid $27.50, with 10 percent going to the agent. Bradbury split the remainder with Hasse. This left him with a little more than $12, not much even in 1941. Yet it was a sale. He was a professional writer.

THE ATTACK ON PEARL HARBOR

In the last month of 1941, a Japanese armada massed some 200 miles (321.8 km) north of Hawaii. In the early morning hours of December 7, squadrons launched from the decks of a half dozen aircraft carriers. The attack on Pearl Harbor,

On December 7, 1941, Japanese forces attacked the U.S. naval base at Pearl Harbor, in Hawaii, bringing the United States into World War II. Here, three U.S. battleships—the USS West Virginia, *the USS* Tennessee, *and the USS* Arizona—*are ablaze from Japanese bombs.*

a U.S. naval base, was both surprising and devastating. Nearly 3,000 Americans lost their lives; much of the country's naval might lay in ruins.

The next day, President Franklin Delano Roosevelt asked the U.S. Congress to approve a declaration of war against Japan. Shortly thereafter, Italy and Germany, Japan's allies, declared war on America. The United States had entered World War II. Ray Bradbury's nightmare was coming true.

Unable to alter those circumstances, Bradbury focused the one thing he could control: writing. He utilized a technique described in Dorothea Brande's 1934 book, *Becoming a Writer*. She offered advice on avoiding the bane of every storyteller: writer's block. In his 1985 mystery *Death is a Lonely Business*, Bradbury's protagonist echoes Brande's advice when he puts a piece of paper in a typewriter and tells police officer and aspiring novelist Elmo Crumley: "Tomorrow morning you get out of bed, walk to the machine, no phone calls, no newspaper reading, don't even go to the bathroom, sit down, type, and Elmo Crumley is immortal."[7]

The Brande method seemed tailor-made for a short story writer such as Bradbury, who could create an entire piece in a single morning. "When I write a short story," he later explained, "I open the trapdoor on the top of my head, take out one lizard, shut the trapdoor, skin the lizard and pin it up on the wall."[8]

In the waning months of 1941, Hasse and Bradbury's collaboration led to two more sales. Despite this, Bradbury ended the partnership. "I discovered that collaborators use each other as crutches and you lean on the other person. You need to learn to walk by yourself. . . . Hasse never forgave me."[9]

While working with Hasse, however, Bradbury acquired an important mentor, a fellow Science Fiction Society attendee named Henry Kuttner. Five years Bradbury's senior, Kuttner was working for a Beverly Hills literary agency when he sold his short story "Graveyard Rats" to *Weird Tales* magazine in 1936.

"I started out in *Weird Tales* [in 1942] with a conventional story called 'The Candle,'" remembers Bradbury. "I couldn't solve the ending. I was clumsy. So [Henry

ttner] said, 'For God's sake, here. Give me your typewriter.' He typed out the last two hundred words as I recall.
And they're still in the story."[10] *Weird Tales* soon became
a regular buyer of Bradbury's work. Bradbury recalled that
Kuttner

> came in one day and said, "Ray, do me a favor." I said,
> "What?" He said, "Shut up." I said, "Why do you say that?"

Did you know...

Weird Tales, the magazine where Ray
Bradbury cultivated his distinctive voice,
began in 1923. According to its Web site, it
"has enjoyed a devoted following for many
decades as the very first magazine of gothic
fantasy, sci-fi, and horror." It introduced
Conan the Barbarian and launched "the
careers of great authors like H.P. Lovecraft,
Ray Bradbury, and Robert E. Howard, Tennessee Williams made his first sale here! . . .
The magazine's influence extends through
countless areas of pop culture: fiction,
certainly, but also rock music, Goth style,
comic books, gaming . . . even Stephen King
has called *Weird Tales* a major inspiration."*

The magazine folded in 1954, but after
several attempts it was reborn in 1988. In
August 2009, *Weird Tales* won its first Hugo
Award, one of the most prestigious honors
in science fiction and fantasy.

*History of *Weird Tales* magazine, http://weirdtales.
net/wordpress/about/history/.

He said, "You go around telling your ideas all the time and you blow the energy, you give away the passion that should go into your writing. So if you're not careful, you're going to throw your career right out the window and you'll never write another story." So he scared me and he was right. It's the best advice I've ever had.[11]

After those early years, Bradbury never divulged details about his next story. Kuttner's advice soon paid dividends. In 1943, he sold 11 short stories. The income from those sales convinced him it was time for him to quit his day job.

Self-employment was a great motivator. In 1944, his first year as a full-time writer, Bradbury sold 18 stories. By writing so many stories he unearthed his distinctive voice—evident in 1942's "The Lake," which first appeared in *Weird Tales*. In an essay published in *Zen in the Art of Writing*, Bradbury remembered:

> I wrote the title "The Lake" on the first page of a story that finished itself two hours later. Two hours after that I was sitting at my typewriter out on a porch in the sun with tears running off the tip of my nose, and the hair on the back of my neck standing up.
>
> Why the arousal of hair and the dripping nose?
>
> I realized I had at last written a really fine story. The first in ten years of writing.[12]

DELIVERANCE AND BREAKTHROUGHS

On July 16, 1942, Bradbury appeared for his physical to determine his eligibility for the draft. He was asked to remove his glasses and read an eye chart. "What chart?" was Bradbury's reply. His poor eyesight earned him a "4-F" designation, which meant he was ineligible for the draft. His nightmare would not come true. He would not die in battle.

Many consider Bradbury a pacifist for not fighting in World War II. Others, however, saw Bradbury's lack of service differently. Former military man Robert Heinlein ended his friendship with Bradbury because he believed he faked the test to get out of fighting. Regardless, the writer contributed to the war effort, volunteering at the Red Cross, for which he wrote promotional materials and advertising.

Bradbury's fan base grew. He also began writing a column for *Weird Tales* as his byline appeared in a range of magazines such as *Captain Future* and *Dime Detective*. Yet the writer worried his career was limited as a "pulp fiction" author. His agent, Schwartz, had no contacts with the better magazines. The short fiction these popular magazines published was widely read by important New York City editors, few of whom would glance at a pulp.

Grant Beach was an old friend who had met Bradbury at Science Fiction Society meetings in the late 1930s. In the mid-1940s, he made two suggestions that altered Ray Bradbury's life. The first was to see a psychiatrist. Arriving at his appointment, the therapist asked Bradbury what he wanted. The author hesitated for only a moment before answering, "I want to be the greatest writer who has ever lived."[13]

Laughing, the psychiatrist advised Bradbury to read about the lives of famous authors, many of whom took much more than a decade to achieve success. "Read their lives," Bradbury remembered him saying, "and you'll understand what writing is, what fame is and all about getting established."[14] So Bradbury did that.

He also followed Beach's second bit of advice. Since Schwartz did not have any connections at "the slicks,"

Beach thought the writer should choose his best, unpublished stories and submit them himself. Here, Bradbury was reluctant. He had done that in high school and succeeded only in acquiring a stack of rejection letters. The odds for success were slim. Bradbury, however, was a far better writer than he had been in high school.

During the summer of 1945, Bradbury submitted "Invisible Boy" to *Mademoiselle*, "One Timeless Spring" to *Collier's*, and "The Miracles of Jane" to *Charmed*. Then he waited.

During a single week in late August, Bradbury received acceptances from all three. It was a nearly unfathomable achievement. His total earnings from the three sales surpassed $1,000—equal to two years of selling newspapers.

During another week in early August 1945, World War II ended. The conflict was brought to a close by a weapon that forever altered everyday life and sparked a surge in science fiction's popularity.

This photo, taken by the U.S. Army Signal Corps, shows the devastation left after the first atomic bomb was dropped on Hiroshima, Japan, on August 6, 1945. Such all-powerful weapons had only been imagined in science fiction stories before World War II; in the postwar years, authors would use these weapons as the backdrop of many post-apocalyptic tales.

6

The Bradbury Chronicles

THE ATTACK BEGAN at dawn. Launched from Tinian island, the *Enola Gay*, an American B-29 Superfortress bomber, flew north by northwest to Japan. Flying at low altitude and avoiding radar, it ascended to 31,000 feet (9,449 meters) before releasing its payload at 8:15 A.M.

It was August 6, 1945. The city of Hiroshima was just waking up. Children were arriving to their first classes of the day. Commuters were riding bicycles to work. Soldiers were performing drills at the parade grounds as the first atomic weapon used in warfare detonated 1,900 feet (579 m) above them.

The atomic bomb, a device based on complex principles unfamiliar to most Americans, did not just help end a long and brutal war. It also marked the birth of the "atomic age." The Hiroshima bomb engulfed the city in a millisecond blast of light and heat. Thousands were instantly incinerated, leaving shadows silhouetted against damaged buildings.

More than 100,000 people died immediately; half the city's population was either killed or injured by the blast. Thousands more died of radiation poisoning in the days and weeks that followed. Why had the United States government and its Allies agreed to use such a devastating weapon? In 1944, just a year earlier, Allied forces had launched a ground invasion along the coast of occupied France. The march to Germany and victory cost tens of thousands of lives on both sides. President Harry S. Truman, hoping to avoid more Allied casualties (which were estimated at around 1 million), gave the order for the attack on Hiroshima. When the Japanese government refused to surrender, another atomic bomb was dropped on the city of Nagasaki four days later. Faced with total annihilation, Japan surrendered. World War II, the most destructive war in human history, was over.

THE WAR'S IMPACT ON SCI-FI

"[World War II] was the first major conflict whose course was determined by science and technology," explains James Gunn is *The Science of Science Fiction Writing*. "It validated those persistent, and often ridiculed SF [science fiction] concepts, the rocket ship and the atom bomb. In the late 1940s and early 1950s, as a consequence, SF proliferated in new magazines, anthologies, and hardcover and soft cover novels."[1]

Just as popular culture was embracing science fiction, Ray Bradbury began writing for popular magazines. Bradbury was a "soft" science fiction writer, more concerned with technology's impact and less with describing technology in precise detail, like "hard" science fiction authors Isaac Asimov and Arthur C. Clarke. While many readers of high-circulation magazines considered Bradbury their favorite science fiction author, most fans of the genre did not consider him a science fiction author at all.

Bradbury was also a genre fan. In 1939, Bradbury wrote August Derleth and Donald Wandrei, who ran Wisconsin-based Arkham House, praising their publication of H.P. Lovecraft's *The Outsider and Others*. In 1945, they published *Who Knocks?*, a book of so-called "weird fiction," which included Bradbury's short story "The Lake." It was the first time a Bradbury story was published in book form. Two years later, when Arkham House published *Dark Carnival*, an entire book of Bradbury's short stories, it marked a clear delineation in Bradbury's career.

By then, Bradbury had moved away from "weird fiction." The year *Dark Carnival* was published, Bradbury's short story "I See You Never" appeared in the pages of the *New Yorker*; the year before his "The Big Black and White Game" was published in *The Best American Short Stories of the Year*.

After his vampire tale "Homecoming" was rejected by the editors at *Weird Tales* for being too quirky, Bradbury submitted it to *Mademoiselle*. There an intern named Truman Capote, who would become a successful writer, rescued it from the slush pile. The story of a child raised by vampires seemed odd for the women's magazine, until the editors decided to use it as a centerpiece for a special

Halloween issue featuring drawings by Charles Addams, the artist who created *The Addams Family*.

Not long after Bradbury's successful placement of "A Timeless Spring" at *Collier's*, he received a letter from a former editor there. Don Congdon had been recently hired as an editor by publisher Simon and Schuster. He loved the writer's work and wanted to know if Bradbury was working on a novel.

Bradbury told him he was not. Yet, he wrote back flattered to be contacted by a major publisher even if he did not have anything to show them.

A STRONG PARTNER

In April 1946, Bradbury was browsing in Fowler Brothers Bookstore in downtown Los Angeles. Dressed in a trench coat on a hot day and lugging a battered briefcase, he looked like a shoplifter to clerk Marguerite McClure. She asked if he needed any help. Tongue-tied in the presence of the stylish and attractive young woman, Bradbury managed to ask if they carried *Who Knocks?* He told her a story of his was in it. Although the shop did not carry it, she tracked the book down after he left.

An only child raised by a successful restaurateur, McClure was fluent in several languages, better read than Bradbury, and having attended UCLA, better educated. Yet she was intrigued. "I was dazzled by the style of the story," she recalled.[2] When a nervous Bradbury returned to ask her out, she accepted. "His energy was enchanting," she remembered. "I had never encountered anyone who could talk like him."[3]

Two months later they were engaged. On September 27, 1947, they were married at the Mount Calvary Church. Ray Harryhausen, the great film producer and special effects creator, was Bradbury's best man; McClure's best friend,

John Nomland, was her "maid" of honor. There were no other friends or family in attendance. At the service's conclusion, Ray Bradbury handed the priest an envelope with $5 in it. The author recalled:

> "What's this for?" he asked.
>   "That's your fee for the ceremony today." Bradbury replied.
>   "You're a writer aren't you? . . . Then you're gonna need this." The priest gave Bradbury his money back.[4]

The priest was right. Bradbury had $8 to his name, including the $5 the priest returned. Soon his wife would be pregnant with their first child. He needed a breakthrough. He needed money.

THE MARTIAN CHRONICLES

When Congdon left Simon and Schuster to become an agent, he asked Bradbury if he needed one. "Yes, I need one," Bradbury wrote back, "but only for a lifetime."[5] (This statement was very nearly true. Congdon would remain the author's agent until Congdon's death at the age of 91 in 2009. Today, Bradbury is represented by Congdon's son Michael.) Although Bradbury had been successfully submitted to "the slicks," Congdon dramatically increased the writer's sales and income as his agent.

Ray Bradbury continued to write, while Marguerite went to work. The income from her job as a secretary helped cover the rent for their tiny apartment at 33 South Venice Boulevard. Although it was an easy stroll from the beach, the neighborhood was quite poor. So were the newlyweds.

Bradbury bought just enough stamps to mail his manuscripts. "Right across from our apartment was a tiny gas station," he remembered. "At the time, there was an outdoor phone booth. So I kept the window open in our front room and when the phone rang, I jumped up and ran across Venice Boulevard and answered the phone and people thought they were calling my home."[6]

His wife never had to worry about money before their marriage. Yet the writer does not recall her complaining. Marguerite believed in her husband. Her belief in him paid early dividends. In 1948, his short story "I See You Never" was included in the year's *Best American Short Story* collection and "Powerhouse" won third place among the annual O. Henry Short Stories (behind Capote, who had rescued "Homecoming" from the slush pile, and Wallace Stegner). Several Bradbury stories were adapted for the radio; he even wrote a few scripts himself. "The Meadow" not only aired on ABC Radio, but was also included in *The Best American One Act Plays of 1947–1948*.

Yet, 1949 began poorly. The editors at Farrar, Straus rejected his short story collection. "They sent it back and said that the writing was not good enough," he recalled. "They said some of the stories were good, but others had overtones of pulp writing. It was a very snobbish letter."[7] But Bradbury's days as a pulp writer were numbered. The appearance of "Black Ferris" in *Weird Tales* in January 1948 marked his last sale to a pulp.

Bradbury knew he had to write a novel in order to make more money. Stories could not keep himself and his family on sound financial footing. He recalled how, in 1944, Henry Kuttner had given him Sherwood Anderson's collection of interconnected stories, *Winesburg, Ohio*. Bradbury imagined a similar work set on Mars. "I decided first of all that there would be certain elements of similarity between the invasion of Mars and the invasion of the Wild West," Bradbury later wrote in an unpublished essay. "I had heard from my father's lips, and my grandfathers, stories of varied adventures in the West, even in the late year of 1908, when things were plenty empty, still and lonely."[8]

For example, in Bradbury's 1948 short story, "And the Moon Be Still as Bright," the Fourth Expedition to Mars encounters a desolate, unpopulated planet. The Martians had succumbed to a plague of chicken pox. Just as Western expansion greatly reduced Native Americans' numbers, explorers from the Earth killed—intentionally or not—the vast majority of Martians.

Around this time, Bradbury got in touch with radio producer Norman Corwin. "I sent Norman a copy of [Bradbury's book of short stories] *Dark Carnival* with a note saying, 'If you like this book half as much as I love your work, I'd like to buy you drinks someday,'" Bradbury told biographer Sam Weller. Corwin called the Bradbury home in Venice Beach a week later and said, "You're not buying me drinks. I'm buying you dinner."[9]

Bradbury's work made a strong impression. "I just felt that this man had a lot of power," the radio producer later told Weller. "Great reserves of power. He was very flexible. He could write what was conveniently called science fiction, he could write poetry, and he had a great sense of humor, which he employed very effectively."[10]

Corwin encouraged the author to visit New York, where most major book publishers were based. There, Bradbury spent a fruitless week meeting with disinterested editors who wanted not stories but a completed novel. Then, as now, short story collections rarely made money. Agent Jim Rutman explains, "We don't really have much choice but to represent talent in whatever form it happens to come. And if it happens to come first in short story collection form, that does not make things easier. . . . It's not fun to call an editor and say, 'What I have for you now—brace yourself—is a collection of short stories.'"[11]

On his final night in New York, Doubleday editor Walter Bradbury asked Ray Bradbury to prepare an outline for a book of Martian stories. He returned to his room at the YMCA. "Air conditioning was still a luxury of some future year," he recalled. "I typed until 3 A.M., perspiring in my underwear as I weighted and balanced my Martians in their strange cities in the last hours before arrivals and departures of my astronauts."[12]

Since his Mars-set short stories were in Los Angeles, he had to construct short descriptions from memory. Inspired by *The Grapes of Wrath*, he later incorporated a similar bridge technique to tie the stories together.

The next day Walter Bradbury liked the writer's outline and asked whether Bradbury had anything else. For decades, Ray Bradbury said he gave the editor *The Illustrated*

Did you know...

The Mars that Ray Bradbury imagined was based more on the ideas of astronomers from the nineteenth century than ones in the twentieth. In the late 1800s, Giovanni Schiaparelli described the network of fine lines he saw on the planet as "canali," meaning a natural channel. Another astronomer, Percival Lowell, who was influenced by Schiaparelli's drawings, concluded that the canals were constructed by intelligent beings. *The Martian Chronicles* features canals, water, and communities of native Martians.

Man. Not until 2006 did biographer Sam Weller publish a different account. "I was wrong about that. My memory was incorrect," Bradbury told Weller. Instead, the second advance was for expanding his short story "The Creatures that Time Forgot" into a 50,000-word novel.[13]

According to notes Weller uncovered, Walter Bradbury did not suggest the title either, although Ray Bradbury gave him the credit. Regardless, the writer left New York with a $1,500 check and a contract for two books. In Los Angeles, the money covered rent and other expenses. One major expense: Marguerite was pregnant.

THE WRITING LIFE

Returning to Los Angeles, Bradbury began riding his bicycle every morning the six blocks to his parents' home, where he used their garage as an office. Back home, Marguerite typed the pages into a final draft. In October 1949, Bradbury sent the manuscript to his editor. The next month, Marguerite went into labor. Lacking a car, the Bradburys made arrangements with their next-door neighbors for help when Marguerite went into labor; it was just after midnight on November 5 when Bradbury pounded on their door. The neighbors drove the Bradburys to Santa Monica Hospital, where Marguerite gave birth to a baby girl at 9:38 A.M. Susan Marguerite Bradbury "does not, alas, resemble in any way a Small Assassin," Bradbury later told August Derleth, the publisher of *Dark Carnival,* alluding to his story about a murderous baby.[14]

Ray Bradbury took an active interest in every aspect of the production of *The Martian Chronicles.* He argued with his editor about what stories to exclude and include. Despite his editor's objections, he succeeded in retaining "Usher II." Bradbury later said the story was a poor fit, and wrote his editor Walter Bradbury admitting he was right: "I should have followed your advice and cut it. . . . It is a good story, but time and again people have mentioned it to me as a lump in the cake frosting. I let my love for the story blind me to its position in relation to the whole. I should have taken advantage of your more objective view."[15]

When *The Martian Chronicles* hit bookstores in 1950, Bradbury's first novel seemed destined for the discount shelf. Books by new authors need word of mouth. In 1950, the best way to get attention was a positive review. According to Bradbury, not a single critic reviewed the book when it was first published because *The Martian Chronicles* was science fiction. Sixty years ago, respected critics in magazines and newspapers did not review science fiction.

Luck, timing, and Bradbury's confident enthusiasm altered the book's downward trajectory. "I was in a bookstore," the author recalled in a 2000 speech:

> I bumped into Christopher Isherwood. I did not know him. I grabbed a copy of my book, I signed it and gave it to him. . . . [t]hree days later, Christopher Isherwood called me and said, "Do you know what you've done?"
>
> I said, "No, what have I done?"
>
> He said, "You've written a remarkable book and I'm going to be the book editor and writer for *Tomorrow Magazine* next October and this will be my first review." So he did a three page review of *The Martian Chronicles* which introduced me to the intellectual world and saved my soul.[16]

Despite the book's success, Bradbury still did not believe the sustained energy he utilized when crafting a short story could be replicated with a novel. Instead, his publisher let him produce another book of short stories. The writer suggested expanding his short story about a man with tattoos covering his body. Every night as he sweats, they come alive and tell their stories. *The Illustrated Man* (1951) utilized this framing device featuring a carnival freak whose tattooed-covered body depicts characters in book's stories.

After *The Illustrated Man*, Bradbury completed *The Golden Apples of the Sun*, a 1953 collection in which the stories were either new or previously published in "the slicks." There was not a single pulp story among them. Ray Bradbury was now coming into his own as a major new author.

In his novel Fahrenheit 451, *Ray Bradbury explored the issue of censorship by imagining a world in which firemen burned books to suppress knowledge. Seen here, a scene from the 1966 film adaptation by French director Francois Truffant.*

7

The Temperature at Which Paper Burns

OVER THE LABOR DAY weekend in 1949, Robert Lilinthal, the head of the Atomic Energy Commission, was vacationing on Martha's Vineyard. It was nearly midnight. He and his wife had just enjoyed a late dinner in nearby Edgartown and were driving back to their second home.

A man stepped from the fog. He had bad news. A U.S. B-29 flying between Alaska and Japan collected an air sample that was consistent with a fission explosion. It was a near certainty that the Soviet Union, America's Cold War adversary, had tested an atomic bomb.

For a few years after World War II, between 1945 and 1949, the United States was the only nation on the planet possessing atomic weapons. Once the Russian test was verified, an arms race began between the United States and the Soviet Union. Over the next decades, each nation produced enough nuclear weapons to kill every person on the planet several times over.

In such a terrifying time, Bradbury's own writing increasingly focused on saving the world. "I was warning people. I was *preventing* futures," he recalled.[1] *The Martian Chronicles* and *The Illustrated Man* included stories about human settlers escaping nuclear apocalypse on their home planet. As the number of nations testing nuclear weapons multiplied, many readers considered such stories predictive of a frightening future.

At the same time, Ray Bradbury was finally ready to write a novel and took his inspiration from something he had seen as a youth. As a teenager, the movies he watched in Los Angeles included introductory newsreels—short black-and-white films that depicted current events around the world. In 1934, while watching footage of Nazi soldiers burning books, he cried. "When Hitler burned a book," Bradbury later wrote, "I felt it as keenly, please forgive me, as his killing a human, for in the long sum of history they are one and the same flesh."[2] During their time in power, the Nazis controlled all information in Germany. Repressive regimes such as the Nazis eliminate anything breeding dissent. As a result, newspapers and other media are strictly regulated. Books—not just books opposed to the party in power, but those that might inspire citizens to picture a better life—are illegal.

In his first true novel, Bradbury envisioned a fireman. This fireman did not put out fires. He started them. He burned books. The idea for the novel grew from five of his short stories he called the "five ladyfinger firecrackers." "The Bonfire," "Bright Phoenix," "The Exiles," "The Pedestrian," and "Usher II" all celebrated individual liberty over the power of a controlling government.[3]

The novel he would later call the "explosion" began in fact as a novella. "The Fireman" was 25,000 words, more than twice as long as most short stories but much shorter than a novel. Unfortunately for the author, he could not sell it. Don Congdon failed to place it with a major magazine; Walter Bradbury passed on publishing the work with Doubleday. He allowed Ray Bradbury to go to another publisher if it was part of a short story collection since Doubleday wanted Bradbury's next novel.

The fact that Doubleday passed on the novella bothered Bradbury. The writer admired Walter Bradbury but had mixed feelings about his publisher. Ray Bradbury believed Doubleday's labeling of his books as science fiction limited their audience.

In 1952, Ian Ballantine and Stanley Kauffman left Bantam Books, which had published paperback reprints of *The Martian Chronicles* and *The Illustrated Man*. Together they began Ballantine Books and agreed to simultaneously offer hardcover and paperback versions of a book including "The Fireman." This was unprecedented.

In exchange, Bradbury received a $5,000 advance, money he sorely needed. In addition to three-year-old Susan, the family now included two-year-old Ramona.

"I had no money to rent a proper office," Bradbury recalled in a speech in 2000. "I had a large family at home and I needed to have a place where I could go for a few hours. I was wandering around the UCLA campus, and I looked down below and I listened and down in the basement I heard this typing."[4]

The room in the library's basement had a dozen typewriters connected to a machine. It released them for a dime. At the end of 30 minutes, the machine locked the typewriter until another dime was inserted. Ray Bradbury had found his office.

WRITING A BOOK ON BURNING BOOKS

"The Fireman" and the book it spawned envisioned a future where books were illegal and televisions dominated homes. Since the lead character, Guy Montag, burns books, "I decided I might well use the temperature at which book paper catches fire," Bradbury recalled. He spoke to professors in chemistry and physics departments at several universities. No one could provide a definitive answer.[5]

"I slapped my forehead and muttered, 'Fool! Why not ask the fire department!'" A call to the downtown station yielded an answer—paper burns at 451 degrees Fahrenheit. "I never bothered to check to see if that was right,"[6] the author admitted.

After reversing the word order (because he liked the way it sounded better), Bradbury had his title: *Fahrenheit 451*. Like *1984* author George Orwell, Bradbury was influenced by images of totalitarian regimes destroying "dangerous books." "After all, *Fahrenheit 451* is all about Russia, and all about China, isn't it?" he remarked during an interview in 1990 with writer Rob Couteau. "And all about the totalitarians anywhere: left or right, doesn't matter; they're book burners; all of them."[7]

Although "The Fireman" and the novel it inspired shared characters and a basic plot, Bradbury consulted the short story as little as possible once he began the novel. "I feared for re-firing the book and re-baking the characters," he remembered. "I am a passionate, not intellectual writer, which means my characters must plunge ahead of me to live the story. If my intellect caught up with them too swiftly, the whole adventure might mire down in self-doubt and endless mind play."[8] Bradbury recalled his passionate sense of play 50 years later.

> I moved [to the library] one day with a bag of dimes and I began inserting dimes into the machine. . . . Can you imagine what it was like to write *Fahrenheit 451* in the library where you could run upstairs and feel the ambience of your beloved writers; and you could take books off the shelf and discover things that you want to put in the book as a quote and then run back down and finish writing another page? So, over a period of nine days I spent $9.80 and I wrote *Fahrenheit 451*.[9]

Montag's conversion from book burner to book believer was powerfully redemptive and echoed the conversion the apostle Paul underwent after being struck blind on the road to Damascus for persecuting Christians. Critics such as Kevin Hoskinson considered *Fahrenheit 451* Bradbury's first "true" novel. Hoskinson explained in his essay "Ray Bradbury's Cold War Novels" that

> many of the stories [in *The Martian Chronicles*] were separately conceived, most of the characters in the finished book are contained within their individual tales and do not cross over into other chapters. In contrast *Fahrenheit 451* is structured as a novel, divided into three chapters; it is set on Earth; it is the story of one central protagonist Guy Montag; and the plot of the novel—Montag's liberation from Captain Beatty and his acceptance of a new purpose in a new civilization—is carefully mapped out.[10]

For an investment of less than $10, Bradbury had produced the book that would cement his reputation. Published on October 19, 1953, *Fahrenheit 451* had a first paperback printing of 250,000 copies. Unlike most popular novels that sell poorly a few years after their publication, sales of *Fahrenheit 451* remained steady. It soon became assigned reading in high school and college classrooms and would go on to sell more than 5 million copies. "I could retire on the royalties of that one book alone," Bradbury admitted two decades after it was published.[11]

Unlike much of Bradbury's work, it was also predictive. Just as Jules Verne in the nineteenth century envisioned technology such as the submarine, the airplane, and the challenges of space travel, biographer Sam Weller notes that *Fahrenheit 451* "predicts, among other things, society's reliance upon television, plasma-screen wall televisions, the invention of stereo headphones (the seashell radio has long been rumored to be the inspiration behind the invention of the Sony Walkman) and even live media coverage of sensationalist news events."[12]

Did you know...

Fahrenheit 451, Ray Bradbury's novel about censorship, was itself censored. "I discovered that, over the years, some cubby-hole editors at Ballantine Books, fearful of contaminating the young, censored some seventy-five separate sections from the novel," a flabbergasted Bradbury wrote in the 1979 coda to *Fahrenheit 451*. The writer was never informed, nor was his permission sought. Instead, he wrote, "Students, reading the novel which, after all, deals with censorship and book-burning in the future, wrote to tell me of this exquisite irony."* The excised passages were restored in subsequent editions.

*Ray Bradbury, *Fahrenheit 451* (New York: Ballantine Books, 1979), p. 177.

MAKING MOVIES

Perhaps more than any other genre, science fiction has benefited from moviemaking's technological breakthroughs. In even the earliest motion pictures, filmmakers sought not just to capture reality but to show the fantastic. In 1902's *A Trip to the Moon*, a slingshot-launched rocket concludes its journey in the unhappy Moon's right eye. "You can do anything in a novel," Ray Bradbury explained to biographer David Mogan, "and most of it you can't do on film because it's too expensive."[13]

In earlier decades, costly special effects meant filmmakers found producing science fiction movies more prohibitively expensive than horror and comedy. Today, however, some of the most expensive and profitable movies of all time are labeled science fiction.

"Genre films often appeal to subconscious anxieties in the audience," film scholar Louis Giannetti explains.

> For example, many Japanese science-fiction films of the 1950s dealt with hideous mutations that resulted from atomic radiation. A number of cultural commentators have remarked on the "paranoid style" of most American sci-fi movies of the 1950s, when the "Red Scare" [fear of Communist infiltration into various aspects of American life] intensified the Cold War atmosphere between the United States and the Soviet Union.[14]

Like the science fiction movies of the 1950s (a genre then growing in popularity), Bradbury crafted stories reflecting the worries of the times. Yet, despite several opportunities, Bradbury resisted working for Hollywood. Bradbury later said that

> the remarkable thing is how long I was able to hold off being tempted by [motion pictures]. . . . I don't want to look upon this as a supreme act of will or integrity or anything because

I imagine it was just fear. Fear can be a very constructive element in one's life, if you are afraid of the right things. . . . I was afraid of the [movie] studios; and luckily I had some good friends who advised me to learn how to write first and then go into the studios later in life.[15]

In 1952, Hal Chester, a movie producer working for Warner Brothers, called Bradbury. Chester was developing a sci-fi movie. When the movie was filmed, Ray Harryhausen would supervise the visual effects.

Excited by the prospect of working with his friend Harryhausen, Bradbury agreed to a meeting. When he arrived, Chester handed Bradbury the script. Bradbury went into another room, sat down, and began to read. He was flabbergasted. The script was almost identical to a short story he had published in the *Saturday Evening Post*. He recalled:

After reading the script, I went out and Hal Chester said, "What do you think? Would you be interested in working on this screenplay?" I said, "Yeah, I would, but incidentally there's a slight resemblance to my story 'The Beast from 20,000 Fathoms.'" His jaw dropped, his eyes bugged out, his wig turned around three times, and then I realized that someone in the studio had "borrowed" my idea and written the script. Then they had called me in, forgetting where they had borrowed the idea and asked me to rewrite it.[16]

When the "error" was pointed out, Bradbury was paid $750 for the rights. The writer felt blessed; usually such "errors" are only resolved through expensive lawsuits. About a month later, he was hired to work on *It Came from Outer Space*, which was advertised as the first 3-D science-fiction horror movie. He was hired to write only a treatment, as the studio did not consider him experienced enough to write a complete script. Earning $300 a week for six weeks of work, Bradbury commuted an hour by bus from his West Los Angeles home to Universal Studios in the San Fernando Valley.

Universal wanted a story about a dangerous space creature attacking the Earth. Bradbury had other ideas. "I wanted to treat the invaders as beings who were not dangerous and that was very unusual," Bradbury explained to biographer Weller. "The only other film like it was *The Day the Earth Stood Still*, two years before. These two films stand out as treating creatures who understand humanity."[17] Bradbury wrote an outline of both the studio's version and his own. He "handed them in and lo and behold they had enough brains to pick my way and I won my point," the writer explained.[18]

During his first summer of writing for the movies, Bradbury earned a pair of rare victories for a screenwriter. Short stories and novels are considered the work of their author. Although people such as publishers, editors, agents, friends, and family help to shape the final product, the novelist receives the credit, and the public considers the writer responsible for the book's success or failure.

Making films is different. Dozens of people—studio executives, producers, writers, actors—help take a movie from idea to completed film. The director usually controls the on-set elements: the director of photography and the camera crew, the art director, production designer, and wardrobe along with actors and other crew members. Once filming begins, the writer's job is often over. Everyone else's is just beginning.

A GREAT WHITE WHALE

"So, when friends used to write to me in my late twenties and early thirties and ask, 'Hey, Ray, when are you going to write your first screenplay?'" Bradbury remembered, "I always wrote back half seriously, half humorously, 'when John Huston offers me a job.'"[19]

In 1951, one of Bradbury's film agents, Ray Stark, arranged a dinner meeting with the great film director John Huston. Sitting down, Bradbury told Huston how much he admired his work and hoped they could someday work together. Then he gave Huston his three published books.

Shortly afterward, Huston left to direct *The African Queen* with Humphrey Bogart and Katharine Hepburn. A week after leaving Los Angeles, Huston wrote Bradbury complimenting his talent, naming several favorites from *Dark Carnival* and promising, "There's nothing I'd rather do than work with you on a picture."[20]

In August 1953, Bradbury learned Huston was in Los Angeles. The author waited all week to hear from him. Frustrated, Bradbury accompanied Harryhausen to one of his favorite places, Long Beach's Acre of Books. When he returned home a few hours later, his wife, Marguerite, told him the director had called. He wanted a meeting. In a 2000 speech, Bradbury remembered that the next day in Huston's hotel room, the director asked him:

> "Ray, what are you doing during the next year?"
>
> "Not much, Mr. Huston. Not much." And he said, "Well, Ray, how would you like to come live in Ireland and write this screenplay of Moby Dick?"
>
> "And I said, 'Gee, Mr. Huston, I've never been able to read the [darn] thing.'"
>
> He'd never heard that before and he thought for a moment and then said, "Well, I'll tell you what, Ray. Why don't you go home tonight, read as much as you can, and come back tomorrow and tell me if you'll help me kill a white whale."[21]

Before heading home, Bradbury stopped at a bookstore to buy a copy of *Moby Dick* so could make notes. Inside, he met someone familiar with Huston, Jigee Viertel, who had been married to Huston collaborator Peter Viertel. She warned him, "John Huston will destroy you if you go on that trip." "Well," Bradbury replied, "He's never met anyone quite like me. . . . Maybe he won't try to destroy me. I'll make do."[22]

That night, Bradbury looked over at his wife. "Pray for me," he asked. When she asked him why, he replied, "Because I've got to read a book tonight and do a book report tomorrow."[23]

Works of art such as paintings and classic literature do not change with each viewing; the person viewing them changes. Bradbury's life was radically different now than it had been during his earlier attempts to read *Moby Dick*. Now 33 years old, Bradbury saw in the novel

> a part of myself, the gift of metaphor. . . . All the early writers in America, Melville and Poe and many of the others wrote in a metaphorical style. You could remember the stories. I raced through the book. I didn't read it. I looked at all the metaphors and I came back the next day and I said, "Yes, I'll do it."[24]

Living at a hotel in Ireland with his family, Bradbury spent six months attempting to find the work's essence. Bradbury says he reread some sections 300 times. After seven months, however, he had still not finished the final third of the script. "I got out of bed one morning in London and I looked in the mirror and I said, 'I am Herman Melville,'" Bradbury recalled. "I sat down at the typewriter and in eight blazing hours I wrote the last forty pages of the screenplay and it all came out right; for that one day, for a few hours, the ghost of Melville was really in me."[25]

From left to right, Gregory Peck, who portrayed Captain Ahab, and Leo Genn, who portrayed Starbuck, talk with their director John Huston on the set of the film Moby Dick. *Ray Bradbury adapted Herman Melville's classic novel into the film's screenplay.*

As author David Mogen explained in *Dwayne's United States Author Series*, "Bradbury's screenplay effectively compresses the action of the novel while preserving its spirit."[26] Racing across town, Bradbury reached Huston and gave the script to the director. After reading it, Huston had one response: "By God, start the cameras."[27]

Bradbury said Huston gave him some feedback, but like most directors Huston did not do any actual writing. Screenplay credits are based upon who actually writes the script. When he returned to the United States, Bradbury learned the movie's credits would read "written by Ray Bradbury *and* John Huston."

The novelist was furious. Sharing credit with the director could affect future assignments. With *It Came from Outer*

Space, Universal had hired him to write a treatment because they did not think he could write a screenplay. If Bradbury now shared the writing credit with Huston, he could be seen as needing a director's "help."

Bradbury appealed to the Screenwriter's Guild, the professional union for movie writers. He submitted 2,000 pages of corrected script, all of the multiple drafts he had written. Three people reviewed the evidence. They unanimously determined Bradbury deserved sole credit. Early advertisements for *Moby Dick* were altered to read: "Written by Ray Bradbury." When Huston returned from Europe, however, he demanded the case be reopened, "because he wasn't there when the decision was reached and he had new evidence. And they re-opened the case," Bradbury fumed. "And that's not allowed."[28]

The writer was unimpressed with the director's new evidence. It mainly consisted of a script Huston went through with red pencil, circling the sections he had written. "What kind of evidence is that?" Bradbury asked in comparison with the multiple drafts he had submitted, including "all my notes and outlines. . . . But I lost. I saw the letters from the second group of judges which said: If judged on material alone we would have to give credit to Bradbury. But the fact that Huston is such a famous director makes us lean over backward."[30]

After Bradbury's fears about writing for a movie studio became a self-fulfilling prophecy, the writer focused on television. Film is considered a director's medium; in television, the writer is usually the boss. Television writers are often employed by the same series for years; new directors are usually hired for each episode. In television, Bradbury would become involved with two programs whose distinctive voice matched his own.

Rod Serling, creator and primary writer for The Twilight Zone, *worked with Ray Bradbury on a number of episodes of the hit television series. Bradbury also introduced Serling to a number of speculative fiction authors whose work could be adapted for television.*

8

The Bradbury Zone

"YOU'RE TRAVELING THROUGH another dimension, a dimension not only of sight and sound, but of mind; a journey into a wondrous land whose boundaries are that of imagination—next stop, the Twilight Zone!" *The Twilight Zone*'s host, creator, and primary writer, Rod Serling, offered that now-famous greeting to viewers in each new episode.

In the late 1950s, it was nearly inevitable that the path of one of the most famous science fiction authors would intersect with an equally famous television writer who embraced science fiction in his career. Debuting in 1959 and airing until 1964 (and in reruns ever since), *The Twilight Zone*'s gothic influences and plot twists recalled Ray Bradbury's stories for *Weird Tales*.

By then Bradbury's family was growing at a pace with his career. His third daughter, Bettina Francion, was born on July 22, 1955; his fourth and last child, Alexandra Allison, was born on August 13, 1958. With four rambunctious daughters, piles of keepsakes, and files of story ideas, Bradbury and his family outgrew their ranch home on 10750 Clarkson Road. In 1958, they moved to a larger three-bedroom house in Cheviot Hills. The West Los Angeles neighborhood was a short distance from Beverly Hills and what would become Century City. It was also not far from Westwood, home of the UCLA campus where Bradbury wrote *Fahrenheit 451*.

Like Bradbury, Serling was a small-town boy who grew up loving pulp magazines. They were both bright, curious boys who lived to talk. Serling's play, *Patterns*, was broadcast on *Kraft Television Theater* in 1955, while the following year's *Requiem for a Heavyweight* on *Playhouse 90* won five Emmy Awards, the highest honor in TV. Yet despite his growing success, Serling encountered numerous obstacles.

Controversial subjects he wrote about were edited by network censors and sponsoring businesses. A cigarette lighter manufacturer advertising on *Requiem for a Heavyweight* even exorcised a character's request for a match!

Science fiction, however, let Serling address issues he could not tackle in a more realistic format. Like Bradbury, Serling's futuristic stories addressed civil rights issues, the environment, and the antiwar movement years before they became national concerns.

Several of Bradbury's stories, including "The Rocket," "Summer Night," and "Homecoming," were adapted for television, but on each of these the author's involvement was limited. In 1955, he authored an episode for *On Camera* titled "The Man," along with episodes for *The Jane Wyman Theatre* and *Steve Canyon*. This limited participation would change when he became involved with Serling's new project.

Serling's contract for *The Twilight Zone* required him to write at least 80 percent of the episodes. He had planned to rely upon unknown writers for the remainder, that is, until 14,000 unsolicited scripts and story ideas poured into his production offices in the first week. So he turned to Bradbury. "Rod told me that he was starting a fantasy series," Bradbury told biographer Sam Weller, "but he didn't really know what he was doing. I invited him over to the house that night."[1]

In his basement office, Bradbury piled book upon book into Serling's arms—offering up works by speculative fiction authors such as Charles Beaumont, Richard Matheson, Ronald Dahl, and John Collier. The writer included his own books as well. "I told Rod, 'After you read these books you will have a complete idea of what your show should be like. Buy some of these stories or hire some of these authors to work for you, because you can't do the whole thing by yourself.'"[2]

The statement was prophetic. "When I saw the pilot episode of *The Twilight Zone*, I thought, 'That looks a little bit like a story from *The Martian Chronicles*. I didn't say anything to Rod. I was embarrassed.'"[3] A month later, Serling called. His wife was reading *The Martian Chronicles* and mentioned similarities between "The Silent Towns" chapter and the *Twilight Zone* pilot, "Where is Everybody?" Serling apologized, offering Bradbury compensation. The writer did not want money and considered it an honest mistake.

Unfortunately, with each new episode, Bradbury began to notice that *The Twilight Zone*'s borrowing had increased. "*Twilight Zone* aficionados would note," Weller writes, "that . . . Ray Bradbury does not have a monopoly on tales of nostalgic Americana."[4] Yet episodes such as "Walking Distance" appeared cribbed from Bradbury's stories. The episode's depiction of time travel was similarly described in his 1957 novel *Dandelion Wine* and even featured a character named Dr. Bradbury. "Bradbury's frustration with what he saw broadcast each week on *The Twilight Zone* is perfectly understandable," Christopher Conlon wrote in *Filmfax Magazine*. "*The Zone* is in fact drenched in Bradburian notions and plot devices, and from the onset Serling himself was well aware of Bradbury's central place in mid-century fantasy fiction."[5]

Bradbury submitted three scripts to *The Twilight Zone*. The first was rejected as too expensive to film; the second was purchased but not produced (again because of the production cost). Finally his third effort, "I Sing The Body Electric," was both purchased and produced. The script

Did you know...

Ray Bradbury was eventually able to see his script of "I Sing The Body Electric" filmed exactly as he wanted. In 1982, his teleplay of "The Electric Grandmother" aired on *NBC Peacock Theatre* and starred Maureen Stapleton. This time it not only concluded as he wanted, but was nominated for an Emmy Award.

depicted a family surviving the mother's death. The father buys a robot grandmother to help the children cope with their grief. The author, however, was dissatisfied with the final product. "They cut out the most important part of the story," Bradbury later complained. "The moment of truth in the story when the grandmother tells them that she is a robot."[6]

Bradbury had more success writing for a television program overseen by one of the era's most successful movie directors, Alfred Hitchcock. When *Alfred Hitchcock Presents* premiered in 1955, Hitchcock had been directing for nearly 30 years. He began with silent films, transitioned to talkies, and helmed such suspense movies as *Rebecca*, *North by Northwest*, and *Rear Window*.

"I'd loved Hitchcock forever and I saw his show and realized we were similar spirits," Bradbury remembered.[7] In 1955, the author adapted his short story "Touched With Fire" for the program. During the program's 1955–1964 run (including 1964's *The Alfred Hitchcock Hour*), Bradbury sold one or two teleplays per year to Hitchcock.

If Hitchcock did not like an idea it was never filmed. The director liked Bradbury's work so much he asked Bradbury to adapt Daphne du Maurier's short story "The Birds." (She had also written the novel *Rebecca* that later became the Hitchcock film.) Bradbury told the director he would love to write the script, but that he would not be able to start for two more weeks. Hitchcock asked why. The author answered that he was already working. For whom, Hitchcock wondered. "For Hitchcock," Bradbury replied. The director looked confused. The writer continued, "I'm working for you already doing a teleplay for your television show. If you'll just wait two weeks, I'll write *The Birds*."[8]

Ray Bradbury browses through a collection of space suits for a possible television series in this 1959 photo. In addition to working with Serling, Bradbury would also write for the television series **Alfred Hitchcock Presents.**

The director would not wait. Evan Hunter, who wrote the bestseller *The Blackboard Jungle* and later authored the 87th Precinct series under the pen name Ed McBain, got the job instead. It was just one job lost. Fortunately, Bradbury was at work on a new book.

DANDELION WINE

While working in television, Bradbury completed *Dandelion Wine,* one of his most beloved books. The story of Douglas Spaulding (whose name comes from Bradbury's middle and his paternal grandmother's maiden name) during the summers of 1928 and 1929, it is in many ways an autobiographical book, a story combining fact and fiction. "The magic of the novel was the magic of memory," Weller writes.[9]

Published in 1957, *Dandelion Wine* was a hybrid novel-short story collection like *The Martian Chronicles* and *The Illustrated Man*. To Bradbury it was

> my celebration, then, of death as well as life, dark as well as light, old as well as young, smart and dumb combined, sheer joy as well as complete terror written by a boy who once hung upside down in trees, dressed in a bat costume with candy fangs in his mouth, who finally fell out of the trees when he was twelve and went and found a toy-dial typewriter and wrote his first "novel."[10]

SPACE RACE

Fictional descriptions of interplanetary travel moved closer to reality at the end of the 1950s. The Union of Soviet Socialist Republics (USSR) won the first leg of the space race, successfully sending the unmanned satellite *Sputnik 1* into orbit in 1957. This milestone, followed by the successful launch of cosmonaut Yuri Gagarin into space on April 12, 1961, was widely viewed with fear in the United States. Americans began to believe that their Cold War rival had overtaken them technologically.

Although the United States did succeed in launching astronaut Alan Shepard into space the next month, his flight was short and suborbital. Gagarin had actually orbited Earth.

On May 25, 1961, President John F. Kennedy challenged the country to devote its energies to "landing a man on the moon and returning him safely to the Earth" before the decade concluded.[11]

On September 12, Kennedy added,

> We choose to go to the moon in this decade . . . not because [it is] easy but because [it is] hard, because that goal will serve to organize and measure the best of our energies and skills, because that challenge is the one that we are willing to accept, one we are unwilling to postpone, and one which we intend to win.[12]

By the end of the 1960s, one out of 10 Americans had some involvement with the space program. Bradbury, the author of the short story "The Rocket Man," was ebullient. "When science fiction seemed almost exclusively a literature of technophiles, Bradbury became a lone symbol of the dangers of technology, even to the point of refusing to drive an automobile or fly an airplane," explains Gary K. Wolfe. "But when science fiction came increasingly to adopt an ambivalent attitude toward unchecked technological progress, Bradbury became an international spokesman for the virtues of spaceflight and technological achievement."[13]

Bradbury worried that his publisher did not share his enthusiasm. After longtime editor Walter Bradbury left Doubleday for Henry Holt, Ray Bradbury wrote his editor's replacement a letter on July 8, 1960, hoping to "find a new publisher who will see me and this fantastic and exciting new Space Age with the same high-spirits in which I approach it. . . . I need a whole company of people to celebrate and be really excited with me about an age I believe is the greatest man ever lived in."[14]

At this point in his career, Bradbury epitomized a successful writer. His books were read worldwide and his short stories eagerly sought by magazine publishers, and both were regularly adapted for film and television. He was a frequent speaker at schools and bookstores across the country; his work was included in more anthologies than any other living author, numbering more than 2,000 by the 1970s. "It is doubtful that the work of any American author has approached the remarkable anthology exposure achieved by Bradbury," offers William F. Nolan.[15]

Most junior high school students read "The Sound of Summer Running," a short story about the magic of new sneakers; others enjoy "All Summer in a Day," depicting a young girl locked in a closet as the rain ends on Venus for the first time in seven years. "More people ask me about that one story than any other," Bradbury said, because it "reveals the dark side in all of us. It makes us feel ashamed."[16]

Ray Bradbury is photographed in 1978. By this point in his career, he had moved away from writing pure speculative fiction and had branched out into writing horror and autobiographical fiction as well.

9

Wicked Games

ARDENT FANS HAD waited for something Ray Bradbury had not produced in half-a-dozen years: a novel. In 1962, their hopes were fulfilled.

Something Wicked This Way Comes combined familiar Ray Bradbury elements in an unfamiliar way. *Fahrenheit 451*, *The Illustrated Man*, and *The Martian Chronicles* were generally categorized as science fiction; *Dandelion Wine* was similarly labeled but Bradbury considered it "autobiographical fiction" despite its occasionally fantastic elements.

With a title taken from the witches' chant in William Shakespeare's *Macbeth*, *Something Wicked This Way Comes* blended science fiction, autobiographical fiction, and elements from tales of terror Bradbury sold to the pulps. It begins as two 13-year-old best friends eagerly await Halloween and their shared birthday. Jim Nightshade is eager to grow up. His best friend and the story's main character, William Holliday, has mixed feelings about the prospect. Like Bradbury, Holliday cherishes his childhood.

Jim's desire to be a different age is shared by several townspeople. He wants to be older. William's father wants to be as young as the other fathers. Of William, he remarks, "He jumps, I creep. How can you get two people together like that? He's too young, I'm too old."[1]

The arrival of "Cooger and Dark's Pandemonium Shadow Show" at three in the morning twists the story. There the funhouse of mirrors is not an entertainment, but a trap. Mr. Electro's electric chair is more preservative than magic. The show's merry-go-round makes the rider younger or older depending upon its rotation. Participants endure unwanted outcomes as the ride lasts longer than they expected.

"The boys and the father provide an effective point of view from which to dramatize the sinister appeal of evil," notes David Mogen, adding, "Bradbury embodies this vision of evil, the true lyrical center of the novel, both in the 'autumn people' themselves and in the entertainments they provide."[2]

The "autumn people's" leader, Mr. Dark, is a devil-like character seeking souls while delivering less than promised. Like Bradbury's Illustrated Man, this carnival's master of ceremonies is decorated with tattoos depicting souls lost to his cunning. Dark's relentless pursuit of the boys (and their souls) drives the novel from nostalgic remembrance toward horror. To many readers, it was Bradbury's first novel best savored late at night—although one interrupted by checks of the locks, the windows, and the closets.

"When I visit schools, kids always ask me, 'What's the scariest book you've ever read?'" says R.L. Stine, the author of numerous books of horror for pre-teens and teens, adding, "I always tell them *Something Wicked This Way Comes*. I still remember how creepy it was."[3]

"As in Bradbury's short fiction, the atmospheric conditions in *Something Wicked* run true to Gothic form," writes Hazel Pierce in the essay "Ray Bradbury and the Gothic Tradition."[4] "Poe is a major link between Ray Bradbury and the gothic tradition. . . . In his reading of Poe, the youthful Bradbury could not have overlooked the awareness of what makes the hair on the back of the neck stand on end."[5]

Like Alfred Hitchcock's *Psycho*, which was released into theaters two years later, Bradbury's novel inspired imitators and homage. Stephen King's first best sellers were labeled horror; like Bradbury, King's stories featured familiar settings and ordinary people faced with extraordinary circumstances. "[W]ithout Ray Bradbury, there is no Stephen King, as least as he grew," King says.[6]

KELLY CONNECTION

Although the story began in the darkest shadows of Bradbury's imagination, *Something Wicked This Way Comes* was in fact inspired by a legendary Hollywood song-and-dance man. Gene Kelly was in his forties and moving away from acting and dancing toward directing when he befriended Bradbury.

In 1955, Ray and Marguerite Bradbury took in a screening of Kelly's movie *Invitation to the Dance* at MGM Studios in Culver City. Missing the bus home, they decided to walk. During the trip, Ray Bradbury confessed to Marguerite that he would give anything to work with Kelly. She suggested he should dig through his files where "you have dozens of ideas stashed away. Find something that strikes you absolutely right . . . and send it over to Gene."[7]

Bradbury listened. He looked through stories, story fragments, and story ideas until he found the script he had adapted from "The Black Ferris," which he described as "the tale of a stage carnival and two small boys and a night with no dawn in sight."[8]

Bradbury gave it to Kelly, who attempted to raise financing for a movie. A month later, Kelly phoned apologizing. He could not get the movie financed. "Sorry?!" Bradbury replied. "Good Lord, I'm proud that you even tried."[9]

ADAPTATION

By the 1960s, numerous filmmakers clamored to transform Bradbury's stories into movies. In 1962, Bradbury collaborated with *Twilight Zone* writer George Clayton Johnson on an animated short film based upon Bradbury's story "Icarus Montgolfier Wright"; the short was nominated for an Academy Award. Then, in 1964, Bradbury funded The

Did you know...

The 1997 edition of *Something Wicked This Way Comes* contains a revised dedication: "With love to the memory of Gene Kelly, whose performances influenced and changed my life."*

*Ray Bradbury, *Something Wicked This Way Comes* (New York: Avon Books, 1997).

Pandemonium Theatre Company to turn his stories into plays. Although it has resided at several locations, the company is still in existence and the writer is still its executive producer.

In 1966, French filmmaker Francois Truffaut directed an adaptation of *Fahrenheit 451*, but creative exhaustion prevented Bradbury from writing the screenplay. He had just turned *Fahrenheit 451* into a play. "He sent me his screenplay. . . . I decided not to read it," Bradbury later told the *Los Angeles Times*. "Invited to London to watch the filming, I refused. . . . By keeping my mouth shut, I gave him license to purify the intent of my book." Avoiding the novel's more fantastic elements, Bradbury says the movie focused on "a man who reads and a book that must be read. Man as lover, book as loved one."[10]

Not all adaptations of his works were as successful. For example, Bradbury felt the filmmakers adapting *The Illustrated Man* in 1969 needed his help. His suggestions were ignored. "The director was a bad director and the producer wrote the screenplay," Bradbury told Mogen. "If they'd asked me to do certain sections over, I could have corrected the script in one day. But they never *asked* that. They were arrogant. They thought they knew everything."[11]

While the movie of *The Illustrated Man* disappointed, the adaptation of Bradbury's short story "In a Season of Calm Weather" almost produced a fistfight. Although Bradbury authored the script, as biographer Sam Weller explains, once shooting began, the director decided to "ad lib the story to give it a more 'natural' narrative flow. It was a crazy, artistic decision with disastrous results."[12]

After a private screening, Weller writes, "When the film was over and the lights came up, Ray turned and pointed to

In July 1969, the Apollo 11 lunar module, **Eagle,** *begins its ascent to rendezvous with the command and service module* **Columbia** *after humanity's first successful lunar landing. After witnessing the Moon landings, Ray Bradbury became more optimistic about mankind's future.*

the director, 'Fire that man.' [The director] jumped to his feet and started after to hit me. People had to get between us so we wouldn't come to blows."[13]

A SMALL STEP

On July 20, 1969, much of the world gathered around their television sets to witness a historic event in human history—the first Moon landing. With the immortal line, "That's one small step for [a] man, one giant leap for mankind," 38-year-old Neil Armstrong descended from the Apollo 11 lunar module onto the surface of the Moon.

To a national audience, Bradbury explained the mission's importance to CBS News reporter Mike Wallace:

This is an effort to become immortal. At the center of all of our religions, all of our sciences, all of our thinking over a good period of years has been the question of death. And if we stay here on Earth we all of us are doomed, because someday the sun will either explode or go out. So in order to ensure the entire race existing a million years from today, a billion years from today, we're going to take our seed out into space and we're going to plant it on other worlds, and then we won't have to ask ourselves the question of death ever again.[14]

In January 1980, Ray Bradbury poses alongside a model of Epcot, a theme park dedicated to technology and innovation at the Walt Disney World Resort in Orlando, Florida, which he helped to design.

10

Live Forever!

RAY BRADBURY DID not like *It's The Great Pumpkin, Charlie Brown*. A fan of *Peanuts* creator and illustrator Charles Schulz, Bradbury had one reason for his dissatisfaction: He wanted to *see* the Great Pumpkin, which never appeared in the cartoon holiday special. It was fall of 1966. The day after Bradbury watched the holiday special, Chuck Jones called. An animator best known for his work on Bugs Bunny and other *Loony Tunes* film shorts, Jones also directed the holiday cartoon adaptation of Dr. Seuss's children's book *How The Grinch Stole Christmas!* Jones shared Bradbury's feelings.

Bradbury had done an oil painting six years earlier, which depicted a tree laden with jack-o'-lanterns instead of leaves. Based on that image, they collaborated on a screenplay called *The Halloween Tree*. Their script detailing a Halloween quest by a group of children went unsold. Then Jones's employer, MGM, stopped making cartoons. The two were also unable to obtain financing elsewhere.

As he had with "Dark Ferris" (which became *Something Wicked This Way Comes*), Ray Bradbury turned the script into a book. He submitted it to Knopf publishing, where editor Bob Gottlieb asked for numerous revisions. Unlike the stereotypical writer upset by suggestions to alter his work, Bradbury quickly made the changes, admitting the book "was much richer than the original screenplay. I added a lot of new material to the book."[1]

His only disappointment was *The Halloween Tree* (1972) being labeled young adult. Bradbury felt it should be marketed to all ages and shelved in both the adult and young adult sections. Bradbury believed that categorizing his work this way limited its audience.

The author refused to be limited by anyone's preconceived notions. Known primarily as a fiction author, he received notice for much of his nonfiction work. In 1970, for example, he wrote an essay for the *Los Angeles Times*'s magazine, *West*, "The Girls Walk This Way; the Boys Walk That Way," which examined the disappearance of town centers as central gathering places. In a later interview, Bradbury blamed cities' failures as the "failure of the mayors and the city councils who don't understand what cities are . . . [m]y dream has been: if they won't do it, some sort of corporate effort has to do it."[2]

Inspired by Bradbury's essay, an architect named Jon Jerde designed the Glendale Galleria, incorporating

Bradbury's themes. Eventually Bradbury collaborated on several Jerde projects, including the Westside Pavilion in Westwood and San Diego's Horton Plaza, with the goal "[t]o build into these arcades twists and turns and upper levels that by their mysteriousness draw the eye and attract the soul."[3]

MAKING MOVIES

Ray Bradbury first met Sam Peckinpah in 1950 when the future director was a University of Southern California film student in his mid-twenties who had boldly knocked on the writer's front door. Twenty-one years later, Peckinpah wanted to direct *Something Wicked This Way Comes*, despite a reputation built on graphically violent pictures such as 1969's *The Wild Bunch*. "I asked Sam, 'How would you make the film?'" Bradbury recalled. The director replied, "Take the book and shove the pages into the camera."[4] Bradbury was convinced.

Unfortunately, like Gene Kelly 15 years before, Peckinpah's quest for financing was ultimately fruitless. In 1977, Bradbury sold the rights to Paramount Studios. Jack Clayton, an associate producer on *Moby Dick*, was hired to produce *Something Wicked This Way Comes*. Already a successful movie director, for 1974's adaptation of *The Great Gatsby*, Clayton knew they needed a good script. "The first script I handed in to Jack was 220 pages," Bradbury remembered. "He made me cut it and cut it and cut it." After several rewrites, "we had a nice script of 120 pages. Perfect. And it was perfect because Jack was patient with me. He was a very bright guy."[5]

Clayton was ready to begin shooting. Unfortunately his bosses, Barry Diller and Michael Eisner, did not see eye-to-eye on the project. Bradbury never learned which one liked it, but their disagreement put the project in limbo. The rights reverted back to the author.

In the meanwhile, in January 1980, NBC aired *The Martian Chronicles* as a three-part miniseries starring Rock Hudson and Roddy McDowall. Following its screening, a reporter asked Bradbury's opinion. His one-word answer? *Boring.* Later, NBC President Fred Silverman asked why he said that. Bradbury asked if he had seen it. After Silverman conceded that he had not, the author advised, "Well you better see it because you've got a boring miniseries on your hands."[6]

Not wanting *Something Wicked* to be equally tedious, Bradbury took his time selling the rights. When Disney purchased them in 1982, the writer was already connected to the company. He had met with founder Walt Disney in 1964 to discuss what would become the Experimental Prototype Community of Tomorrow, better known as Epcot. A World's Fair that would never close, it would feature cultural pavilions combining education and entertainment.

The Walt Disney Company also finally got Ray Bradbury on an airplane. In October 1982, he reached Epcot's grand opening by taking a train to New Orleans, a limousine to Tallahassee, Florida, and, after the limo broke down, a $200 taxicab ride to Orlando. After the celebration, he told the Disney people that "God's been whispering to me, 'Fly, Dummy! Fly!'" Disney provided a flight home. "I took my first flight and I didn't panic," Bradbury remembered. "I discovered that I wasn't afraid of flying. I was afraid of me. I was afraid that I would run up and down the aisles screaming for them to stop the plane."[7]

The experience meant Bradbury and his wife began flying regularly. It also meant that he developed an affinity for Disney. Still, when he learned the company was planning to hire someone other than Clayton to direct *Something Wicked* because they felt he was too old to direct a movie for young people, "I told them, it's very simple, if you don't use him, I won't sell you the script."[8]

The day before principal photography, Clayton handed Bradbury the script. A writer Clayton used on other films, John Mortimer, had completely rewritten it. "He was a fine writer, but he didn't know fantasy," Bradbury decided.[9] Clayton, however, ignored Bradbury's suggestions. Despite feeling betrayed, Bradbury loved watching as a company with a long history of turning fictional fantasy into film reality constructed Green Town. "It was still my film. It was my book," he remembered.[10]

After a preview screening left the audience bored, Disney's head Ron Miller summoned Bradbury to his office. The writer was ready. "Rebuild the sets," he advised. "Rehire the actors. I'll rewrite the script. I'll make a new ending."[11] The rewritten script, author David Mogen notes:

> effectively captures the spirit of the book, though it has not proven a commercial success. Yet those who are impatient with the novel's ornate style might well prefer the movie. . . . [E]ssentially Bradbury's screenplay simplifies the story, dropping scenes that do not translate effectively into film, fusing characters and events in new combinations to advance the narrative more efficiently.[12]

Bradbury often mentioned wanting to direct, but did not expect his chance to come the way it did. "Jack [Clayton] was there but he was mainly on the side. It was all a very strange situation," Bradbury admitted. "In the end we spent five million dollars redoing everything that Jack Clayton did wrong. Unofficially, I became the director of the film."[13]

After a creative lifetime watching his stories radically altered for the big and small screens, Ray Bradbury was given a rare opportunity in the mid-1980s. Larry Wilcox, an actor then known for his role on the television series *CHiPs*, had a production company that courted the writer. In 1985, *The Ray Bradbury Theatre* premiered on HBO. During the next seven years (the last six on cable channel USA), Bradbury served as executive producer on all 65 episodes. Each episode was based on one of his stories; each one was introduced by the writer—just like Rod Serling and Alfred Hitchcock. Over its run, the series was nominated for 31 Cable Ace Awards, winning 12.

NEW NOVELS

In 1985, Bradbury delighted his fans with his first novel in many years. *Death is a Lonely Business* was similar to stories Bradbury sold to the pulps in the 1940s, with a writer instead of a detective as the main character. Based upon his own experiences in Venice Beach, California, the

Did you know...

A new version of *Fahrenheit 451*, produced by actor Mel Gibson's Icon Productions, is listed as in preproduction, according to the Internet Movie Database. Although a cast or start date for filming has not been announced, Frank Darabont is attached as the writer and director. Darabont is the writer-director of *The Shawshank Redemption* and *The Mist*, both adaptations of novellas written by Stephen King.

book substituted dark and dreary urban streets typical of the pulps for the fog-bound seaside community.

Bradbury followed *Death is a Lonely Business* with *Green Shadows, White Whale* in 1992. A semi-autobiographical novel, *Green Shadows, White Whale* was inspired by his time working with director John Huston.

Bradbury also expanded earlier stories. *From the Dust Returned* (2001) was a vampire story featuring the Uncle Einar character depicted in a short story of the same name some 60 years earlier. The writer also finished work on a sequel to *Dandelion Wine*, a book he had written in the 1950s. *Farewell Summer* (2006) had resulted from advice Bradbury received from his editor Walter Bradbury. In the summer of 1956, after his review of the novel, Walter Bradbury wrote the author, "If you just take hold of this book by the ears and rip it apart, it will fall into two halves. Every other chapter should go out, and the remaining chapters will fall into place. They will be your first book, and every other chapter will be your sequel."[14]

In 2006, the author wrote in the "Afterword" in *Farewell Summer* that "it has taken all these years for the second part of *Dandelion Wine* to evolve to the point where I felt it was correct to send out to the world."[15]

LOSSES AND GAINS

At the beginning of the twenty-first century, age-related health issues plagued the Bradburys. Ray Bradbury's love for sweets, along with his increasing alcohol dependency, contributed to a stroke in late 1999. Because of his limited mobility, he could no longer type and began dictating stories to daughter Alexandra.

On November 24, 2003, Marguerite died from lung cancer. The loss devastated her husband. "During her illness,

In 1997, Ray Bradbury takes a break from signing his new book **Quicker Than The Eye,** *in Cupertino, California. Bradbury believes that humans will return to the Moon, then go to Mars, and eventually to other stars.*

and in the time since, for the first time in seventy years my demon has lain quiet within me," Bradbury wrote in the "Introduction" to his 2004 short story collection *The Cat's Pajamas.* "My muse, my Maggie, was gone and my demon did not know what to do. As the days passed, and then the weeks, I began to wonder if I would ever write again; I was unaccustomed to waking in the morning and not having my private theatre acting out its ideas inside my head."[16]

Yet writing was a comfort, a familiar retreat into a magical world. Eventually, Bradbury wrote again.

BIOGRAPHY

In 2000, journalist Sam Weller's profile of Bradbury for the *Chicago Tribune Magazine* led to his writing of an authorized biography of the writer, *The Bradbury Chronicles*. Unlike most books written about Ray Bradbury, Weller's benefited from unprecedented access. Over the course of five years, the journalist not only interviewed Bradbury, his family, friends, and colleagues, but also went through Bradbury's file cabinets and collections.

Published in 2005, the biography corrected many errors of fact, some unintentionally created by Bradbury. These include his recollections regarding the genesis of *The Martian Chronicles* and *The Illustrated Man*. Interviews with Bradbury in *The Bradbury Chronicles* even contradict details about writing a script for Gene Kelly that are found in "A Brief Afterword" in current editions of *Something Wicked this Way Comes*.

In the final pages of *The Bradbury Chronicles*, Bradbury wrote in the essay "All's Weller That Ends Weller":

> The lessons that can be learned from this book are simply that if you write for a single day, at the end of the day you're pleased that you wrote something . . . at the end of the year if you can look back on 365 days of writing every single day, a feeling of optimism rewards you. . . . I cannot help but recommend Sam Weller's patient recitation of my early days to show other young talents how to keep so busy that they won't be able to recognize their failures or inadequacies. . . . Beyond that, Weller's discussion of accomplishments and rewards that came late in life is most pleasant, but never the less of no practical use to anyone planning a future of writing.[17]

HEADING TO THE FUTURE

On July 19, 1979, Ray Bradbury was brought to Cape Canaveral, Florida, as part of ABC's *Infinite Horizon: Space Beyond Apollo*, which examined the space program on the Moon landing's tenth anniversary. "The launch sites were abandoned," he remembered. "The very spot where the rockets lifted off. Abandoned in place. In other words, we had given up on the moon."[18]

Over the next three decades, the space shuttle fleet, built beginning in the late 1970s, would be utilized for satellite repair and space station construction. Many, including Bradbury, believe this program has not captured the public's imagination as the lunar landings had in the 1960s.

At the same time, Bradbury's politics had evolved. His displeasure with President Lyndon Johnson's handling of the Vietnam War led him to leave the Democratic Party. In the 1980s, his support for Republicans increased; he noted in one interview that he believed President Ronald Reagan, a Republican, would "probably go down in history as the most important president of the last century. Because he did in the communist empire."[19]

Bradbury had reason to admire another president. In 2004, President George W. Bush proposed that the United States send manned rockets to the Moon by 2020. It was planned that human beings would land on Mars sometime after that. In order to finance the explorations, NASA would end the shuttle program in 2010. The same year that Bush made his proposal, he presented Ray Bradbury with the National Medal of Arts, the country's highest honor conferred onto an individual artist.

On the fortieth anniversary of Apollo 11, in 2009, Buzz Aldrin, the second man to set foot on the Moon, expressed his support for such a trip to Mars. "What I want to do is to encourage people to look very carefully at what is the destination that we are setting a goal for," he told CBS's Bob Schieffer.[20] According to a CBS poll taken at the time of the anniversary, about 51 percent supported manned trips to Mars, despite the economic challenges gripping the nation.

Many supporters of the space program and science fiction fans, however, were disappointed when President Barrack Obama did not use the anniversary of the first lunar landing to renew Bush's pledge to expand manned space exploration; in fact, Obama canceled Project Constellation, the Bush-era program that would have returned Americans to the Moon, in favor of having private companies build the next generation of space vehicles. Instead, Obama hopes 2020 will be the date when the United States will have "the highest college graduation rates of any country on Earth."[21]

LEGACY

Decades after his first books were published, Ray Bradbury's work continues to inspire. In his book *Danse Macabre*, Stephen King wrote:

> I remarked to an interviewer once that most great writers have a curious childish look to their faces, and that this seems even more pronounced in the faces of those who write fantasy. It is perhaps most noticeable in the face of Ray Bradbury, who retains very strongly the look of the boy he was in Illinois.[22]

At 90 years old, Bradbury still embraces the wonder of his childhood, the feeling that surrogate Douglas Spaulding expressed by saying "I'm alive," an unsurprising revelation except that, "Thinking about it, noticing it is new."[23] It is that revelation that inspires the expression "Live Forever," the words of an author whose words endure as he enters his tenth decade.

CHRONOLOGY

1920   Ray Douglas Bradbury is born on August 22 to Leonard and Esther Marie Bradbury in Waukegan, Illinois.

1920–1926   The Bradbury family resides in Waukegan; in 1926, Ray's one-year-old sister, Elizabeth, dies.

1926–1927   The family moves to Tucson, Arizona; Ray begins reading comic strips.

1927   Family returns to Waukegan.

1928   Ray discovers an abandoned issue of *Amazing Stories* in his grandparents' home, beginning his love of pulp fiction.

1929   Ray begins reading and collecting *Buck Rogers in the 25th Century* comic strips.

1931   Upset that he has read all of Edgar Rice Burroughs's Mars series, Ray and his friend Bill Arno write their own "sequel" on butcher paper.

1932   The family returns to Tucson; Ray acts in school plays and performs on a radio station.

1933   The Bradbury family returns to Waukegan.

1934   Family relocates to Los Angeles, where Ray Bradbury will live for the rest of his life.

1934–1938   Attending Los Angeles High School, Ray attends tapings of *The Burns and Allen Show*; he is unsuccessful at placing his fiction in either national magazines or his high school literary magazine; comedian George Burns does use a small comedy bit of Ray's, and his hometown newspaper publishes one of his poems.

1937   Bradbury joins the Los Angeles Science Fiction Society.

1938   Bradbury graduates from Los Angeles High School; his first published short story, "Hollerbochen's Dilemma," appears in the Los Angeles Science Fiction Society's fanzine.

1938–1942   Bradbury sells newspapers for the *Herald Express*, the *Los Angeles Herald Examiner*'s afternoon edition.

1939 Bradbury publishes the magazine *Futuria Fantasia* and attends the World Science Fiction Convention in New York City.

1941 Collaborating with Henry Hasse, Ray Bradbury sells his first short story, "Pendulum"; following the Japanese sneak attack on Pearl Harbor, the U.S. enters World War II, but poor eyesight prevents Bradbury from serving in the military.

1942 Selling short stories regularly to *Weird Tales*, *Super Science Stories*, and other pulps, Bradbury stops selling newspapers and works full-time at the job he will hold for the rest of his life: writer.

1945 Bradbury sells to the "slicks," receiving acceptances for "Invisible Boy" from *Mademoiselle*, "One Timeless Spring" from *Colliers*, and "The Miracles of Jane" from *Charmed* in a single week.

1946 Bradbury meets Marguerite McClure in a downtown L.A. bookstore.

1947 Bradbury's first book of short stories, *Dark Carnival*, is published. Marries Marguerite McClure on September 27; he becomes a client of literary agent Don Congdon, who will represent Bradbury for the next six decades.

1949 Bradbury earns a $750 advance for *The Martian Chronicles*; on November 5, his daughter Susan Marguerite is born.

1950 *The Martian Chronicles* is published.

1951 *The Illustrated Man* is published; Bradbury's daughter Ramona is born.

1952 Bradbury writes "The Fireman," a novella that will inspire *Fahrenheit 451*; he writes a script treatment for the movie *It Came from Outer Space*.

1953 *Fahrenheit 451* is published; Bradbury lives in Ireland with his family for six months while writing the screenplay for the film *Moby Dick*.

1955 *The October Country*—primarily rewritten stories from *Dark Carnival*—is published; Bradbury's daughter Bettina Francion is born; Bradbury begins writing for television, including for *Alfred Hitchcock Presents*.

1957 *Dandelion Wine* is published.

1958 Bradbury makes his last appearance in *Best American Short Stories* with "The Day It Rained Forever"; his fourth and final daughter, Alexandra Allison, is born.

1960 Bradbury leaves his longtime publisher Doubleday.

1962 *Something Wicked This Way Comes* is published.

1964 Bradbury founds The Pandemonium Theatre Company, where he will produce plays for more than 40 years.

1966 The film version of *Fahrenheit 451*, directed by Francois Truffaut, is released.

1972 *The Halloween Tree* is published.

1980 NBC's *The Martian Chronicles*, a three-part miniseries, airs; Bradbury calls it boring.

1984 The movie version of *Something Wicked This Way Comes* is released.

1985 *Death is a Lonely Business* is published.

1985–1992 *The Ray Bradbury Theatre*, 65 episodes based on Ray Bradbury short stories, airs.

1992 *Green Shadows, White Whale*, Bradbury's semi-autobiographical account of working on *Moby Dick*, is published.

1999 Bradbury suffers a stroke.

2003 Marguerite Bradbury dies from lung cancer on November 24.

2004 Bradbury receives the National Medal of Arts from President George W. Bush.

2005 *The Bradbury Chronicles*, the only authorized biography of Ray Bradbury, is published.

2010 The fiftieth anniversary of the publication of *The Martian Chronicles* is marked; Bradbury turns 90 years old.

NOTES

Chapter 1

1 Ray Bradbury, "Acceptance speech upon receiving the Medal for Distinguished Contributions to American Letters," National Book Awards ceremony, November 15, 2000. http://www.raybradbury.com/awards_acceptance.html.

2 Damon Knight, "When I Was in Kneepants: Ray Bradbury," in *Modern Critical Views: Ray Bradbury*. ed. Harold Bloom (Philadelphia: Chelsea House Publishers, 2001), p. 4.

3 Bradbury, "Acceptance speech."

4 Ibid.

5 Ibid.

6 Ibid.

7 Ibid.

Chapter 2

1 Ray Bradbury, *Dandelion Wine* (New York: Bantam, 1975), pp. x–xi.

2 Ray Bradbury, *The October Country* (New York: William Morrow, 1999), p. ix.

3 Sam Weller, *The Bradbury Chronicles: The Life of Ray Bradbury* (New York: Harper Perennial, 2005), p. 25.

4 Bradbury, *The October Country*, p. x.

5 Ibid.

6 Weller, *The Bradbury Chronicles*, p. 37.

7 Stephen King, *Danse Macabre* (New York: Berkley Books, 1981), p. 326.

8 "Tucson Post World War II Residential Subdivision Development, 1945–1973," *Prepared for the City of Tucson Urban Planning and Design Development*. http://0-www.worldbookonline.com.millennium.newport.lib.ca.us/advanced/website?id=http://www.ci.tucson.az.us/.

9 Ray Bradbury, *The Martian Chronicles* (New York: Bantam Books, 1979), p. 18.

10 Weller, *The Bradbury Chronicles,* p. 47.

11 Robert A. Heinlein, *Science Fiction Writers of the Golden Age*, ed. Harold Bloom (New York: Chelsea House Publishers, 1995), p. 111.

12 Matthew J. Bruccoli, preface to *The Great Gatsby*, by F. Scott Fitzgerald (New York: Charles Scribner's Sons, 1992), p. x.

13 Ray Bradbury, *Zen in the Art of Writing* (Santa Barbara, Calif.: Capra Press, 1989), p. xi.

14 David Mogen, *Ray Bradbury* (Boston: Twayne Publishers, 1986), p. 3.

15 Weller, *The Bradbury Chronicles*, p. 199.

Chapter 3

1 Sam Weller, *The Bradbury Chronicles: The Life of Ray Bradbury* (New York: Harper Perennial, 2005), p. 72.

2 Ibid., p. 76.

3 Ibid., p. 79.

4 Ray Bradbury, *Fahrenheit 451* (New York: Ballantine Books, 1953), p. 190.

5 *Contemporary Authors Online*, Gale, 2009. Reproduced in *Biography Resource Center*. Farmington Hills, Mich.: Gale, 2009.

7 "Ray Bradbury Online Quotations," Ray Bradbury Online. http://www.spaceagecity.com/bradbury/quotes.htm.

8 Weller, *The Bradbury Chronicles*, pp. 82–83.

9 Ibid., p. 83.

10 Anne Lamott, *Bird by Bird* (New York: Pantheon Books 1994), p. 157.

11 Weller, *The Bradbury Chronicles*, p. 104.

12 Ibid., p. 85.

13 Ibid.

14 Ibid., p. 86.

15 Ibid., p. 82.

16 Ibid., p. 81.

Chapter 4

1 Sam Weller, *The Bradbury Chronicles: The Life of Ray Bradbury* (New York: Harper Perennial, 2005), p. 89.

2 Natalie Goldberg, *Writing Down the Bones* (Boston: Shambhala, 1986), p. 48.

3 Weller, *The Bradbury Chronicles*, p. 89.

4 Ibid., p. 73.

5 Ray Bradbury, "The Crowd," *The October Country* (New York: William Morrow, 1955), pp. 183–184.

6 Strunk, William Jr., and E.B. White, *The Elements of Style*, 4th Ed. (New York: Longman, 2000), pp. 72, 74–75.

7 Weller, *The Bradbury Chronicles*, p. 9.

8 James Gunn, *The Science of Science Fiction Writing* (Lanham, Md.: Scarecrow Press, 2000), p. 65.

9 Ibid.

10 Ibid., p. 66.

11 Ibid., p. 68.

12 David Mogen, *Ray Bradbury* (Boston: Twayne Publishers, 1986), p. 19.

13 Ray Bradbury, *Zen in the Art of Writing* (Santa Barbara, Calif.: Capra Press, 1989), p. 127.

14 Weller, *The Bradbury Chronicles*, p. 100.

Chapter 5

1 Sam Weller, *The Bradbury Chronicles: The Life of Ray Bradbury* (New York: Harper Perennial, 2005), p. 78.

2 David Mogen, *Ray Bradbury* (Boston: Twayne Publishers, 1986), p. 8.

3 Ray Bradbury, *Zen in the Art of Writing* (Santa Barbara, Calif.: Capra Press, 1989), p. 14.

4 Weller, *The Bradbury Chronicles*, p. 209.

5 Bradbury, *Zen in the Art of Writing*, p. 4.

6 Stephen King, *On Writing* (New York: Pocket Books 2000), p. 159.

7 Ray Bradbury, *Death is a Lonely Business* (New York: Alfred A. Knopf, 1985), p. 86.

8 Weller, *The Bradbury Chronicles*, p. 176.

9 Ibid., p. 107.

10 Mogen, *Ray Bradbury*, p. 9.

11 Ibid.

12 Bradbury, *Zen in the Art of Writing*, p. 15.

13 Weller, *The Bradbury Chronicles*, p. 120.

14 Ibid.

Chapter 6

1 James Gunn, *The Science of Science Fiction Writing* (Lanham, Md.: Scarecrow Press, 2000), p. 69.

2 Sam Weller, *The Bradbury Chronicles: The Life of Ray Bradbury* (New York: Harper Perennial, 2005), p. 137.

3 Ibid.

4 Ibid., p. 148.

5 Ibid.

6 Ibid., p. 151.

7 Ibid., p. 152.

8 Ibid., pp. 155–156.

9 Ibid., pp. 145–146.

10 Ibid.

11 Jofie Ferrari-Adler, "Agents & Editors," *Poets & Writers* 37, Issue 3 (May/June 2009), pp. 48–49.

12 Weller, *The Bradbury Chronicles*, p. 155.

13 Ibid., p. 156.

14 Ibid., p. 160.

15 Ibid., p. 182.

16 Ray Bradbury, "Acceptance speech upon receiving the Medal for Distinguished Contributions to American Letters," National Book Awards ceremony, November 15, 2000. http://www.raybradbury.com/awards_acceptance.html.

Chapter 7

1 David Mogen, *Ray Bradbury* (Boston: Twayne Publishers, 1986), p. 83.

2 Sam Weller, *The Bradbury Chronicles: The Life of Ray Bradbury* (New York: Harper Perennial, 2005), p. 199.

3 Ibid.

4 Ray Bradbury, "Acceptance speech upon receiving the Medal for Distinguished Contributions to American Letters," National Book Awards ceremony, November 15, 2000. http://www.raybradbury.com/awards_acceptance.html.

5 Weller, *The Bradbury Chronicles*, p. 205.

6 Ibid., p. 206.

7 Rob Couteau, "The Romance Of Places: An Interview With Ray Bradbury," *Paris Voice* (November

1990). http://www.tygersofwrath.com/bradbury.htm.

8 Weller, *The Bradbury Chronicles*, p. 205.

9 Bradbury, "Acceptance speech."

10 Kevin Hoskinson, "Ray Bradbury's Cold War Novels," in *Modern Critical Views: Ray Bradbury*, ed. Harold Bloom (Philadelphia: Chelsea House Publishers, 2001), pp. 125–126.

11 Weller, *The Bradbury Chronicles*, p. 209.

12 Ibid.

13 Mogen, *Ray Bradbury*, p. 140.

14 Louis Giannetti, *Understanding Movies*, 5th Ed. (Englewood Cliffs, N.J.: Prentice Hall, 1990), p. 329.

15 Mogen, *Ray Bradbury*, p. 135.

16 Weller, *The Bradbury Chronicles*, p. 190.

17 Ibid., p. 191.

18 Mogen, *Ray Bradbury*, p. 136.

19 Ibid.

20 Weller, *The Bradbury Chronicles*, p. 178.

21 Bradbury, "Acceptance speech."

22 Weller, *The Bradbury Chronicles*, p. 211.

23 Bradbury, "Acceptance speech."

24 Ibid.

25 Ibid.

26 Mogen, *Ray Bradbury*, pp. 136–137.

27 Bradbury, "Acceptance speech."

28 Mogen, *Ray Bradbury*, p. 137.

29 Ibid.

Chapter 8

1 Sam Weller, *The Bradbury Chronicles: The Life of Ray Bradbury* (New York: Harper Perennial, 2005), p. 251.

2 Ibid.

3 Ibid., p. 253.

4 Ibid., p. 254.

5 Ibid.

6 Ibid., p. 261.

7 Ibid., p. 237.

8 Ibid., p. 238.

9 Ibid., p. 243.

10 Ray Bradbury, *Dandelion Wine* (New York: Bantam, 1975), p. xii.

11 President John F. Kennedy, "Speech Delivered Before a Joint Session of Congress," May 25, 1961. http://www.jfklibrary.org/Historical+Resources/Archives/Reference+Desk/Speeches/JFK/Urgent+National+Needs+Page+4.htm.

12 President John F. Kennedy, "Address at Rice University on Nation's Space Effort," September 12, 1962. http://www.jfklibrary.org/Historical+Resources/Archives/Reference+Desk/Speeches/JFK/003POF03SpaceEffort09121962.htm.

13 David Mogen, *Ray Bradbury* (Boston: Twayne Publishers, 1986), p. 95.

14 Weller, *The Bradbury Chronicles*, p. 257.

15 Ibid., p. 296.

16 Ibid., pp. 251–252.

Chapter 9

1 Ray Bradbury, *Something Wicked This Way Comes* (New York: Avon Books, 1962), p. 90.

2 David Mogen, *Ray Bradbury* (Boston: Twayne Publishers, 1986), p. 120.

3 Sam Weller, *The Bradbury Chronicles: The Life of Ray Bradbury* (New York: Harper Perennial, 2005), p. 249.

4 Hazel Pierce, "Ray Bradbury and the Gothic Tradition" in *Modern Critical Views: Ray Bradbury*. ed. Harold Bloom (Philadelphia: Chelsea House Publishers, 2001), p. 69.

5 Ibid., p. 59.

6 Weller, *The Bradbury Chronicles*, p. 153.

7 Bradbury, *Something Wicked This Way Comes*, p. 292.

8 Ibid.

9 Ibid.

10 Ray Bradbury, "Fahrenheit on Film," *Los Angeles Times*, November 20, 1966.

11 Mogen, *Ray Bradbury*, p. 138.

12 Weller, *The Bradbury Chronicles*, pp. 281–282.

13 Ibid., p. 282.

14 Weller, *The Bradbury Chronicles*, p. 283.

Chapter 10

1 Sam Weller, *The Bradbury Chronicles: The Life of Ray Bradbury* (New York: Harper Perennial, 2005), p. 287.

2 Rob Couteau, "The Romance Of Places: An Interview With Ray Bradbury," *Paris Voice* (November 1990). http://www.tygersofwrath.com/bradbury.htm.

3 Weller, *The Bradbury Chronicles*, p. 293.

4 Ibid., p. 305.

5 Ibid., p. 306.

6 Ibid., p. 301.

7 Ibid., p. 304.

8 Ibid., p. 307.

9 Ibid.

10 Ibid., p. 309.

11 Ibid.

12 David Mogen, *Ray Bradbury* (Boston: Twayne Publishers, 1986), pp. 139–140.

13 Weller, *The Bradbury Chronicles*, p. 309.

14 Ibid., p. 242.

15 Ray Bradbury, *Farewell Summer* (New York: William Morrow, 2006), p. 210.

16 Ray Bradbury, *The Cat's Pajamas* (New York: William Morrow, 2004), p. xv.

17 Ray Bradbury, "All's Weller that Ends Weller," in *The Bradbury Chronicles: The Life of Ray Bradbury*, Sam Weller (New York: Harper Perennial, 2005), p. 5.

18 Weller, *The Bradbury Chronicles*, p. 300.

19 Couteau, "The Romance Of Places."

20 CBS News, "Buzz Aldrin, From the White House to Mars," July 20, 2009. http://www.cbsnews.com/

blogs/2009/07/20/politics/
politicalhotsheet/entry5175707.
shtml?tag=contentMain;content
Body.

21 CBS News, "Obama Hails
Apollo 11 Astronauts," July 20,
2009. http://www.cbsnews.com/
blogs/2009/07/20/politics/political-
hotsheet/entry5175254.shtml?tag=
contentMain;contentBody.

22 Stephen King, *Danse Macabre*
(New York: Berkley Books, 1981),
p. 326.

23 Ray Bradbury, *Dandelion Wine*
(New York: Bantam, 1975),
p. 26.

WORKS BY
RAY BRADBURY

1947 *Dark Carnival*

1950 *The Martian Chronicles*

1951 *The Illustrated Man*

1953 *Fahrenheit 451*; *The Golden Apples of the Sun*

1955 *The October Country*; *Switch On the Night*

1957 *Dandelion Wine*

1959 *A Medicine For Melancholy*

1962 *Something Wicked This Way Comes*; *R Is For Rocket*

1964 *The Machineries of Joy*

1966 *S Is For Space*; *Twice 22*

1969 *I Sing the Body Electric*

1972 *The Halloween Tree*; *The Wonderful Ice Cream Suit and Other Plays*

1976 *Long After Midnight*

1977 *Where Robot Mice and Robot Men Run 'Round in Robot Towns*

1980 *The Stories of Ray Bradbury*

1984 *A Memory of Murder*

1985 *Death Is a Lonely Business*

1989 *Zen in the Art of Writing*

1990 *A Graveyard For Lunatics: Another Tale of Two Cities*; *Classic Stories Volume One*; *Classic Stories Volume Two*

1992 *Green Shadows, White Whale*

1996 *Quicker Than The Eye*

1997 *Driving Blind*; *Dogs Think That Every Day Is Christmas*

2001 *From the Dust Returned*

2002 *One More For the Road*

2003 *Let's All Kill Constance*; *Bradbury Stories: 100 of His Most Celebrated Tales*; *The Best of Ray Bradbury: The Graphic Novel*

2004 *The Cat's Pajamas*

2006 *Farewell Summer*

POPULAR BOOKS

THE BEST OF RAY BRADBURY: THE GRAPHIC NOVEL

In the 1950s, several Bradbury stories were used by comic book publishers without authorization. Instead of suing, Bradbury contacted them and gave permission for his work to be used (although he did, of course, want to be paid). *The Best of Ray Bradbury: The Graphic Novel* represents Bradbury's ongoing quest to get his work to the widest possible audience.

DANDELION WINE

Although often labeled as science fiction, this book contains few elements of traditional sci-fi (or fantasy). Instead it is a nostalgic look at early adolescence drawn from many of the writer's memories of his own Illinois hometown.

DEATH IS A LONELY BUSINESS

Based upon Bradbury's own experiences as a struggling pulp writer, this writer-as-detective story was his first full-length novel in 20 years.

FAHRENHEIT 451

Perhaps Bradbury's most studied work, this story of a fireman who burns books stands with Aldous Huxley's *Brave New World* and George Orwell's *1984* as an important work about totalitarian regimes. The writer's first "true" novel, it reflects his love for books and libraries.

FAREWELL SUMMER

As the writer notes, some books came quickly—the novella that led to *Fahrenheit 451* was finished in nine days. *Farewell Summer*, a sequel to *Dandelion Wine*, was completed 50 years after the original.

FROM THE DUST RETURNED

This work sprang from the stories Bradbury wrote in the 1940s, including "Homecoming." Part gothic tale of the undead and part celebration of the writer's own unconventional family members, *From the Dust Returned* is a poetic tale of the supernatural.

THE HALLOWEEN TREE

Inspired by Bradbury's disappointment with a Peanuts holiday special, this short novel follows a group of children on a quest for the origins of Halloween.

THE MARTIAN CHRONICLES

Connecting previously published Mars-set stories with brand new ones, Ray Bradbury's first successful science fiction book covers themes such as racism and environmental and atomic destruction. In the 2000 edition, dates are pushed back from 1999 to 2030 because he wanted to encourage people to go to Mars.

THE OCTOBER COUNTRY

This collection features early short stories that Bradbury sold to the pulps. Although many of them were collected in *Dark Carnival*, the writer rewrote them for this book.

SOMETHING WICKED THIS WAY COMES

As nostalgic as *Dandelion Wine* and as in love with books as *Fahrenheit 451*, this is Bradbury's only novel of true horror. Many of today's horror and thriller writers cite it as an early influence.

POPULAR CHARACTERS

DOUGLAS SPAULDING

A stand-in for Ray Bradbury, the 12-year-old's description of a magical and magic-infused summer in 1928 in *Dandelion Wine* offer fiction readers as much insight into the author as any biography.

GUY MONTAG

"It was a pleasure to burn. It was a pleasure to see things eaten, to see things blackened and *changed*." So begins *Fahrenheit 451*, the story of literature's most famous fireman. Montag is a book burner, until he actually reads one and wonders why he is burning them.

WILLIAM HALLOWAY

He is not in a hurry to grow up. He does not ache for change, to be younger or older. He embraces the joy of the present and perhaps this is what saves his soul from the clutches of Mr. Dark in *Something Wicked This Way Comes*.

THE WRITER

The unnamed protagonist of *Death is a Lonely Business* survives on the meager sales of pulp stories in Venice Beach, California, in the 1940s while dealing with murders and a long distance relationship with a girlfriend in Mexico.

MAJOR AWARDS

1948 "Powerhouse" earns third place in the O. Henry Prize competition.

1953 *Fahrenheit 451* wins a gold medal from the Commonwealth Club of California.

1954 Bradbury wins the National Institute of Arts and Letters award for his contribution to American literature.

1974 Bradbury is given a Writers Guild Award.

1977 He wins a World Fantasy Award for lifetime achievement.

1985 Bradbury is given a Body of Work Award by the PEN organization.

2000 He receives a medal for "Distinguished Contribution to American Letters" from the National Book Foundation.

2001 Bradbury is a Bram Stoker Award nominee in the novel category from the Horror Writers Association for *From the Dust Returned*.

2003 He is given a star on the Hollywood Walk of Fame.

2004 Bradbury receives the National Medal of the Arts.

2007 He is honored with a special citation for distinguished career by the Pulitzer Board.

BIBLIOGRAPHY

Books

Bloom, Harold, ed. *Modern Critical Views: Ray Bradbury*. Philadelphia: Chelsea House Publishers, 2001.

———. *Science Fiction Writers of the Golden Age*. New York: Chelsea House Publishers, 1995.

Bradbury, Ray. "Introduction: Alive and Kicking and Writing." In *The Cat's Pajamas*, p. xv. New York: William Morrow, 2004.

———. "Just This Side of Byzantium: An Introduction." In *Dandelion Wine*, pp. x–xi. New York: Bantam , 1975.

———. "A Conversation with Ray Bradbury." In *Fahrenheit 451,* p. 190. New York: Ballantine Books, 2003.

———. "Afterword: The Importance of Being Startled." In *Farewell Summer*, p. 210. New York: William Morrow, 2006.

———. "Homesteading the October Country, An Introduction." In *The October Country*, p. ix. New York: William Morrow, 1999.

———. *Zen in the Art of Writing*. Santa Barbara, Calif.: Capra Press, 1989.

Bruccoli, Matthew J. "Preface." In *The Great Gatsby,* by F. Scott Fitzgerald. New York: Charles Scribner's Sons, 1992.

Giannetti, Louis. *Understanding Movies*, 5th Ed. Englewood Cliffs, N.J.: Prentice Hall, 1990.

Goldberg, Natalie. *Writing Down the Bones*. Boston: Shambhala, 1986.

Gunn, James. *The Science of Science Fiction Writing*. Lanham, Md.: Scarecrow Press, 2000.

Herken, Gregg. *Brotherhood of the Bomb: The Tangled Lives and Loyalties of Robert Oppenheimer, Ernest Lawrence and Edward Teller*. New York: Henry Holt, 2002.

King, Stephen. *Danse Macabre.* New York: Berkley Books, 1981.

———. *On Writing.* New York: Pocket Books 2000.

Lamott, Anne. *Bird by Bird.* New York: Pantheon Books, 1994.

Mogen, David. *Ray Bradbury*. Boston: Twayne Publishers, 1986.

"Ray Bradbury." In *Concise Dictionary of American Literary Biography: Broadening Views, 1968–1988*. Farmington Hills, Mich.: Gale Research, 1989.

"Ray Bradbury." In *Contemporary Novelists*, 7th ed. Farmington Hills, Mich.: St. James Press, 2001.

"Ray Bradbury." in *Contemporary Popular Writers*. Farmington Hills, Mich.: St. James Press, 1997.

"Ray Bradbury." in *St. James Encyclopedia of Popular Culture*. 5 vols. Farmington Hills, Mich. St. James Press, 2000.

"Ray Bradbury." in *St. James Guide to Horror, Ghost & Gothic Writers*. Farmington Hills, Mich.: St. James Press, 1998.

Strunk, William Jr., and E.B. White. *The Elements of Style*, 4th Ed. New York: Longman, 2000.

Weller, Sam. *The Bradbury Chronicles: The Life of Ray Bradbury*. New York: Harper Perennial, 2005.

Periodicals

Bradbury, Ray. "Fahrenheit on Film." *Los Angeles Times*, November 20, 1966.

Couteau, Rob. "The Romance Of Places: An Interview With Ray Bradbury." *Paris Voice*, November 1990. Available online. URL: http://www.tygersofwrath.com/bradbury.htm.

Ferrari-Adler, Jofie. "Agents & Editors." *Poets & Writers* 37, Issue 3 (May/June 2009).

Speeches

Ray Bradbury. "Acceptance speech upon receiving the Medal for Distinguished Contributions to American Letters." National Book Awards Ceremony, November 15, 2000. Available online. URL: http://www.raybradbury.com/awards_acceptance.html.

Web Sites

BBC, "History of World War II." Available online. URL: http://www.bbc.co.uk/history/worldwars/wwtwo/.

BBC, "The Ending of World War One, and the Legacy of Peace." Available online. URL: http://www.bbc.co.uk/history/worldwars/wwone/war_end_print.html.

BBC, "The Rise of Adolf Hitler." Available online. URL: http://www.bbc .co.uk/history/worldwars/wwtwo/hitler_01.shtml.

CBS News, "Buzz Aldrin, From The White House To Mars" Available online. URL: http://www.cbsnews.com/blogs/2009/07/20/politics/ politicalhotsheet/entry5175707.shtml?tag=contentMain;contentBody Mars.

CBS News, "Obama Hails Apollo 11 Astronauts." Available online. URL: http://www.cbsnews.com/blogs/2009/07/20/politics/politicalhotsheet/ entry5175254.shtml?tag=contentMain;contentBody.

CBS News, "Poll: Americans Say U.S. Should Go To Mars." Available online. URL: http://www.cbsnews.com/blogs/2009/07/20/politics/ politicalhotsheet/entry5173978.shtml?tag=contentMain;contentBody.

Energy Quest, "The Energy Story." Available online. URL: http://www .energyquest.ca.gov/story/chapter13.html.

Henry Hasse. Available online. URL: http://feedbooks.com/author/897.

John F. Kennedy Presidential Library and Museum, May 25, 1961 speech before Congress. Available online. URL: http://www.jfklibrary.org/ Historical+Resources/Archives/Reference+Desk/Speeches/JFK/ Urgent+National+Needs+Page+4.htm.

John F. Kennedy Presidential Library and Museum, September 12, 1962 speech at Rice University. Available online. URL: http://www .jfklibrary.org/Historical+Resources/Archives/Reference+Desk/ Speeches/JFK/003POF03SpaceEffort09121962.htm.

Ray Bradbury Home Page. Available online. URL: http://www.raybradbury .com.

Ray Bradbury Online, "The Quotable Bradbury." Available online. URL: http://www.spaceagecity.com/bradbury/quotes.htm.

National Aeronautics and Space Administration, "The Decision to Go to the Moon." Available online. URL: http://history.nasa.gov/moondec .html.

U.S. Department of Energy, Office of History & Heritage Resources, "The Manhattan Project." Available online. URL: http://www.cfo.doe.gov/ me70/manhattan/hiroshima.htm.

Weird Tales, History of *Weird Tales* Magazine. Available online. URL: http://weirdtales.net/wordpress/about/history/.

FURTHER READING

Bradbury, Ray. *Zen in the Art of Writing.* Santa Barbara, Calif.: Capra Press, 1989.

Goldberg, Natalie. *Writing Down the Bones.* Boston: Shambhala, 1986.

King, Stephen. *Danse Macabre.* New York: Berkley Books, 1981.

———. *On Writing.* New York: Pocket Books 2000.

Lamott, Anne. *Bird by Bird.* New York: Pantheon Books, 1994.

Mogen, David. *Ray Bradbury.* Boston: Twayne Publishers, 1986.

Weller, Sam. *The Bradbury Chronicles: The Life of Ray Bradbury.* New York: Harper Perennial, 2005.

PICTURE CREDITS

INDEX

ABOUT THE CONTRIBUTOR

Born in Boston, Massachusetts, and raised in Vermont, **JOHN BANKSTON** began writing articles while still a teenager. Since then, more than 200 of his articles have been published in magazines and newspapers across the country, including the *Tallahassee Democrat*, the *Orlando Sentinel*, and *The Tallahassean*. He is the author of more than 60 biographies for young adults, including works on scientist Stephen Hawking, anthropologist Margaret Mead, author F. Scott Fitzgerald and actor Heath Ledger. He lives in Newport Beach, California.